Perfection!

2009 NATIONAL CHAMPIONS

Celebrating a perfect ending to another championship season for the Alabama Crimson Tide

The Birmingham News

MOBILE PRESS-REGISTER

The Huntsville Times

www.kcisports.com

Graphic design by Elizabeth Chick
Cover design by Scott Walker
Cover photo by Bill Starling
Printed in the United States of America

ISBN 978-09843882-1-9 (soft cover)
ISBN 978-09843882-0-2 (hard cover)

This book is available in quantity at special discounts for your group or
organization. For further information, contact:
KCI Sports Publishing
3340 Whiting Ave., Suite 5
Stevens Point, WI 54481
(217) 766-3390 voice
(715) 344-2668 fax

www.kcisports.com

Alabama head coach
Nick Saban is dunked
with gatorade during the
BCS National Champion-
ship Game at The Rose
Bowl in Pasadena, Calif.,
Thursday, Jan. 7, 2009.

STAFF PHOTO/
BILL STARLING

Preface...

Bama fans filled the Rose Bowl with a thundering rendition of "Rammer Jammer" as confetti fell on the heads of jubilant players, many of them in tears. Nick Saban, the head coach and grand architect of an undefeated season, hoisted the crystal football signifying the Crimson Tide's 13th national title.

Perfection!

Up in the press box, writers from *The Birmingham News*, *The Huntsville Times*, and *Mobile Press-Register* were penning the last and best chapter about a remarkable season-long journey.

The top stories from newspaper editions published across Alabama the next morning, as well as stories chronicling the facts and emotions of all 14 Alabama wins, have been gathered here for Crimson Tide followers to savor.

The 12 reporters and columnists featured in this book have more than 200 years of combined experience covering Alabama football. Many of them were there to witness Alabama's last national championship 17 years ago.

The Alabama Crimson Tide was college football's finest in 2009-10. Here, in one book, is the finest collection of stories and photos about this unbeatable team.

- Ricky Mathews
January 7, 2010

Ricky Mathews is president of Alabama Advance newspapers. The group includes *The Birmingham News* and *The Huntsville Times* as well as the *Mobile Press-Register*, where Mathews also serves as publisher.

The Birmingham News   MOBILE PRESS-REGISTER   The Huntsville Times

Foreword...

Seventeen Years...

In some ways it seems like the blink of an eye; in others, it seems too long since the University of Alabama Crimson Tide has worn the crown of national champion.

On this day, I feel the same joy and exhilaration for those happy warriors in the Rose Bowl as I did that night 17 years ago when we whipped Miami in the Sugar Bowl to claim Alabama's last national championship.

And as the game unfolded, I couldn't help but think of the similarities between the two teams.

--Of our coach, Gene Stallings; how he demanded the best from each of us. And now Nick Saban and his insistence on poise, determination, toughness, responsibility and character. Core values don't change. They won a championship then, and they won it in 2010.

--Of the great defenses. The debates may go on forever about which is the best. Maybe that's just part of the fun: the good-natured arguments of whether it's Copeland and Curry or McClain and Cody. I don't know. But I do know that I'd be equally proud to claim membership with either group.

--Of players who stood up to be counted when the need arose. I remember the 1994 Georgia game when we were way behind and things looked bleak. I had a great night and we came back to win. After the game someone asked me about my performance and I said that I just wanted to thank Jesus Christ because I'd had so many criticisms through the season, adding that "the Lord says in the Bible 'If you just humble yourself, therefore under His mighty hand, He will life you up in due time,' and this has been due time for me." So many players on this great team have experienced their due time this year, rising up, shouldering the responsibility, when they were needed most.

What great memories they made. Of Mark Ingram taking over the South Carolina game. Of Julio Jones, Trent Richardson and Roy Upchurch making play after play on the climactic final drive against Auburn. Of Greg McElroy building confidence out of a mid-season slump. Of Terrence Cody's big paw slapping down two Tennessee field goal tries. Of Marquis Johnson knocking away pass after pass in the South Carolina game. Rolando McClain's masterful calling of defensive alignments. Young linebackers like Nico Johnson stepping up to fill the massive hole left by the injured Dont'a Hightower. And Brandon Deaderick, only days after being shot in an attempted robbery, stepping onto the field against Virginia Tech.

I could go on and on.

This championship did not just happen on the floor of the Rose Bowl Thursday night, however. Having been there, I know it began much earlier. It began with consistent goals, consistent demands and great leadership by Nick Saban and the men who work for him.

It began with conditioning, both mental and physical, that gave players the desire, the ability and the will to win.

It grew as those players believed in what they were being asked to do, took responsibility for their actions, the actions of their fellow players, and ownership of the team.

Sometimes, no matter how hard you try, how well prepared you are or how much you want something, things don't work out as you hope. As Coach Saban said just a few weeks ago, Even the best can still get whipped.

But I believe that good fortune favors the best prepared, and I believe that there is a time for all things.

The boys of the Crimson Tide believed in their ability, worked hard to be ready and believed in their mission. This was their due time.

Congratulations and thanks for a spectacular and perfect season!

Roll Tide!

Jay Barker
Quarterback, 1992 National Championship Team

Alabama linebacker Rolando McClain (25) Alabama offensive lineman D.J. Fluker (76) Alabama running back Mark Ingram (22) Alabama defensive lineman Marcell Dareus (57) and Alabama defensive back Javier Arenas (28) hold the BCS National Championship trophy after defeating Texas 37-21 at The Rose Bowl in Pasadena, Calif., Thursday, Jan. 7, 2009.

STAFF PHOTO/ BILL STARLING

table of contents

bcs national
texas

championship

CRIMSON TIDE `37`

LONGHORNS `21`

01.07.10 | 7 p.m. | Rose Bowl Stadium | Pasadena, CA

Alabama running back Mark Ingram (22) runs for a first down past Texas defender Earl Thomas (12).

STAFF PHOTO/ BUTCH DILL

Perfection!

Historic Rose Bowl victory clinches Alabama's
13th National Title

By GENTRY ESTES

A soaked Alabama coach Nick Saban wore a jacket as he held a coveted crystal football above his head Thursday night.

When that moment is remembered from this point on, let his attire be proof of the cool breeze flowing into a warm Rose Bowl from the East. It was almost as if the elated folks back home were saying hello.

"This is something that is special for the state of Alabama," Saban said. "It means a tremendous amount for all of us in the state of Alabama and for the University of Alabama to win the BCS national championship."

Alabama is back on top of the college football world, traveling to the West Coast to beat Texas 37-21 and claim the program's first national championship in 17 years and the 13th in the history of Crimson Tide football.

Cue the celebrations.

"This is the epitome," Crimson Tide quarterback Greg McElroy said. "It's such an amazing feeling. I'm so glad to be able to add to the storied history of Alabama football."

"Some people dream and never get to accomplish that dream," Alabama senior tailback Roy Upchurch said. "Tonight my dreams came true."

The blue-collar formula that has become a trademark of this inspired Crimson Tide season was again the backdrop for its conclusion, with the running game and defense allowing Alabama to survive a back-and-forth, unpredictable game.

The top-ranked Crimson Tide (14-0) seized control by outscoring the second-ranked Longhorns 24-0 in the second quarter. But this much-anticipated BCS title tilt — while no less special for Alabama — will be widely remembered for the one star player not on the field.

Texas senior quarterback and Heisman Trophy finalist Colt McCoy was knocked out of the game with a right shoulder injury after five plays, giving way to inexperienced true freshman backup Garrett Gilbert for the remainder of the game.

Gaining nothing on a running play, McCoy was hit in the right side by Alabama defensive end Marcell Dareus, falling awkwardly.

"I really didn't try to hit him that hard," Dareus said. "I didn't want to hurt him. It's a part of the game. I didn't try to hurt him."

McCoy then exited the game and returned to the locker room, not able to return to the season's biggest contest.

2009 national

Alabama head coach Nick Saban holds up the coach's trophy after defeating Texas to win the BCS National Championship Game.

STAFF PHOTO/ BILL STARLING

TEAM	1ST	2ND	3RD	4TH	FINAL
ALABAMA	0	24	0	13	37
TEXAS	6	0	7	8	21

Attendance — 94,906 Rose Bowl Stadium

SCORING SUMMARY

UT — H Lawrence 18 yd field goal, 10 plays, 36 yards, TOP 3:50
UT — H Lawrence 42 yd field goal, 4 plays, 5 yards, TOP 1:07
UA — M Ingram 2 yd run (L Tiffin kick), 7 plays, 57 yards, TOP 3:27
UA — T Richardson 49 yd run (L Tiffin kick), 2 plays, 49 yards, TOP 0:45
UA — L Tiffin 26 yd field goal, 6 plays, 20 yards, TOP 1:51
UA — M Dareus 28 yd interception return (L Tiffin kick)
UT — J Shipley 44 yd pass from G Gilbert (H Lawrence kick) 5 plays, 59 yards, TOP 1:47
UT — J Shipley 28 yd pass from G Gilbert (G Gilbert pass), 9 plays, 65 yards, TOP 4:58
UA — M Ingram 1 yd run (L Tiffin kick), 3 plays, 3 yards, TOP 1:01
UA — T. Richardson 2 yd run (L Tiffin kick failed), 3 plays, 27 yards, TOP 1:01

TEAM STATISTICS

	UA	UT
FIRST DOWNS	16	15
NET YARDS RUSHING	205	81
NET YARDS PASSING	58	195
COMPLETIONS-ATTEMPTS-INT	6-12-1	17-42-4
TOTAL OFFENSE YARDS	263	276
PENALTIES: NUMBER-YARDS	5-38	8-77
PUNTS-YARDS	7-261	8-343
PUNT RETURNS: NUMBER-YDS-TD	3-19-0	0-0-0
KICKOFF RETURNS: NUMBER-YDS-TD	3-19-0	6-106-0
POSSESSION TIME	33:39	26:21
SACKS BY: NUMBER-YARDS LOST	1-14	5-33
FIELD GOALS	1-2	2-2
FUMBLES: NUMBER-LOST	1-1	1-1

INDIVIDUAL OFFENSIVE STATISTICS

Rushing: UA — M Ingram 22-116; T Richardson 19-109; R Upchurch 2-9; G McElroy 7 (-27)
UT — T Newton 14-39; D Monroe 3-33; J Childs 1-8; F Whittaker 1-5; C Johnson 3-2; C McCoy 1-0; G Gilbert 5 (-6)

Passing: UA — G McElroy 6-11-0, 58; P Fitzgerald 0-1-1
UT — G Gilbert 15-40-4, 186; C McCoy 2-2-0, 9

Receiving: UA — T Richardson 2-19; M Ingram 2-12; J Jones 1-23, M Maze 1-4
UT — J Shipley 10-122; M Goodwin 3-70; T Newton 2-2; M Williams 1-4; D Buckner 1 (-3)

INDIVIDUAL DEFENSIVE STATISTICS

INTERCEPTIONS: UA — J Arenas 2-3; M Dareus 1-28; T King 1-0   UT — B Gideon 1-0

SACKS: UA — E Anders 1
UT — L Houston 1; S Kindel 2.5; K Robinson .5; S Acho 1

TACKLES: UA — E Anders 6-1; M Barron 5-1; R Green 4-2; J Arenas 4-1; R McClain 2-2 J Chapman 3-0; K Jackson 2-1; C Reamer 2-1; T Cody 1-2
UT — L Houston 8-2; S Kindle 6-2; K Robinson 3-4; R Muckelroy 6-0; E Thomas 5-1; S Acho 4-2; B Gideon 2-4; C Brown 2-1; A Williams 2-1

champions!

Texas quarterback Colt McCoy (12) is injured on a sack by Alabama defensive lineman Marcell Dareus (57) and Alabama defensive back Kareem Jackson (3).

STAFF PHOTO/ BUTCH DILL

"That's a hit I've taken over and over in my life," McCoy said, "and playing this game, I know you're going to get hit. But I guess I got hit the right way. I'm not in pain, but my arm's dead. It feels like I slept on my arm, woke up and it's just dead."

"As much as I enjoy winning," Saban said, "you hate to see a great competitor who's had a great career not be able to play in a game he's worked his entire career to be a part of."

But Texas (13-1), which appeared down for the count without its star quarterback, charged back with two TDs in the second half, forcing Alabama's defense into a series of big plays to hold on in the final moments.

"They made a game of it," Crimson Tide left guard Mike Johnson said. "They got close, but our defense stepped up."

McElroy threw only 11 passes, while Alabama's Heisman Trophy-winning tailback Mark Ingram rushed for 116 yards and two touchdowns on 22 carries — earning offensive MVP honors — and tailback Trent Richardson added 109 yards and two touchdowns on 19 carries.

While Texas' offense couldn't manage a first down in its first four possessions after McCoy's injury, Alabama began to roll through the nation's top-rated rushing defense.

Defensively, the Crimson Tide forced five turnovers, including three to ice the game in the final minutes and a 28-yard interception return by Dareus — the game's defensive MVP — with three seconds remaining in the first half.

Gilbert wound up 15-for-40 for 186 yards and four interceptions, but he found Jordan Shipley for 44- and 28-yard touchdown strikes in the second half to allow the Longhorns to close to 24-21 with 6:15 to play.

Texas retained possession near the three-minute mark, but on that drive's second play, linebacker Eryk Anders blitzed and blindsided Gilbert to force a fumble that UA's Courtney Upshaw recovered at the Longhorns' 3-yard line.

Alabama then began a celebration that included a Gatorade bath for Saban, who becomes the first coach in history to win BCS titles at two schools.

"I wished they'd do water. The Gatorade is awful sticky," Saban said. "But I'm a lot happier with a bath than if I didn't get one, I'll tell you that."

THE COACHES' TROPHY

Hobbled Colt

By MARK McCARTER

Five plays into the game, Texas quarterback Colt McCoy was knocked from the game with a right shoulder injury after a tackle by Marcell Dareus.

"I wasn't," Dareus pleaded, "trying to hurt him."

It left McCoy with an arm that felt "just dead."

A case can be made that the Longhorn offense was left the same way. McCoy, an All-American and Heisman Trophy finalist, never returned. Texas almost never looked like a national contender.

"He's a great football player. It's obvious that it hurt them," said Alabama defensive end Brandon Deaderick after the Tide's 37-21 win in the BCS National Championship Game. "We can't help we knocked him out of the game. It's just the luck of the draw.

"It's unfortunate for him," Deaderick said, "but one player doesn't make a whole team."

Enter Garrett Gilbert, who found an Alabama defense that "imposed our will on them" in the first half, according to Courtney Upshaw.

As Alabama coach Nick Saban left the field at halftime, he said Texas "got us a little off-balance on defense, because they have a completely different plan for what they are doing (with Gilbert in the game). But we'll get it worked out."

Pardon?

At that point, Alabama already owned an 18-point lead. Gilbert was 1-for-10 for the half with two interceptions. Texas had converted only one of eight third downs.

Though Gilbert showed more poise in the second half and the Texas coaching staff showed more confidence in him, his two touchdown passes to Jordan Shipley wouldn't be enough.

"That quarterback, I really don't know who he is," said Tide defensive end Lorenzo Washington. "But he's going to be a great player. They're not going to be hurting too bad next year when Colt leaves."

But on this night, Texas was hurting.

"I think it was a huge factor," said defensive back Javier Arenas. "It was Colt McCoy. One of the best quarterbacks in the country. When you don't have him in there, it makes it that much easier for the defense."

"When he came out, I didn't know he was hurt until two plays later. I don't know exactly what happened because he's such a great player," said linebacker Corey Reamer. "Our chances were good either way, whether he was in or out. You saw us make plays."

"I think it was a big factor. It took away the running pass from the quarterback," said cornerback Kareem Jackson. "The guy that stepped in did a good job still.

"Football is football. Regardless of who is in there, if he plays or if he doesn't play, we came out and we played hard.

"Regardless of who was at quarterback," Jackson said, "I think we were the better team tonight."

Defense and national titles: Together, a Bama tradition

By KEVIN SCARBINSKY

This is the way Alabama wins a national championship. This is the way Alabama has always won national championships.

First, with a bang, then a whimper.

The names change.

The pain, for the other team, remains the same.

"This game was true Alabama football," said former linebacker DeMeco Ryans, a blast from the recent past who came to bask.

"Defense wins championships. The defense stepped up big-time and made it happen for us."

There were plays to be made before and after, including an old-fashioned goal-line stand, but Alabama beat Texas 37-21 to win the 2010 BCS Championship Game because of two clean, old-fashioned licks.

Marcell Dareus delivered the first one, in the first quarter, as Texas threatened to score a quick touchdown and take control.

Colt McCoy absorbed the blow, on his throwing arm, as he turned an option keeper toward the end zone. The senior leader, who shouldered a massive burden all year, couldn't recover from it.

Don't question his toughness.

Applaud Alabama's.

Eryk Anders landed the knockout blow, in the final minutes, as Texas mounted a championship-style comeback, pulled to within three points and took possession.

Anders came off the edge to separate McCoy's understudy, Garrett Gilbert, from the ball and Texas from its last, best hope.

Given the way Gilbert grew up as time grew short, there's no telling how it would've been different had

Texas quarterback Garrett Gilbert (3) is
sacked by Alabama's Javier Arenas (28)
and Rolando McClain (25).

STAFF PHOTO/ BILL STARLING

McCoy been able to go the distance.

No doubt, someone on the Alabama defense would've made a play to save the day.

Dareus is a sophomore defensive end, and Anders plays that position as a senior. Neither player could be considered a star, at least not yet in the case of Dareus, the game's defensive MVP.

Both players can call themselves champions.

National champions.

It's an Alabama tradition.

"The message tonight was do what we do and be who we are," coach Nick Saban said.

Dareus and Anders got the message. They followed in the marauding footsteps of John Copeland and Eric Curry, the bookend defensive ends who wreaked havoc en route to the 1992 national title.

The entire Alabama defense carried on a legacy that includes the most famous goal-line stand in college football history, the one that stopped Penn State in its tracks in the 1979 Sugar Bowl.

This stand lasted three downs instead of four, and it did yield points, in the form of a field goal. But coming after an ill-conceived fake punt blew up, that stand set a tone.

The final score doesn't reflect it, but this was a defensive struggle, a battle of wits and grit between the master Saban and his star student, Texas defensive coordinator Will Muschamp.

The final margin doesn't reflect it, but this was a struggle, period.

Two late Alabama touchdowns, set up by the defense with turnovers and cashed in by an otherwise sluggish offense, obscured that fact as much as a Gatorade bath turned Saban's bright, white coaching shirt a lovely shade of pink.

It takes a strong man to wear pink. The first coach to win a national championship at two different schools since the AP started its poll in 1936 is as strong as they come.

It takes strong men to wear crimson because those jerseys bear the added weight of 12 national champions who came before.

This is Alabama football. Again.

At its best, it doesn't get any stronger than this.

Alabama running back Mark Ingram)22) celebrates after scoring a touchdown.

STAFF PHOTO/ BILL STARLING

With five takeaways, Tide's defense rules

By DON KAUSLER JR.

Not once but twice, in the opening minutes of the game, Texas got the ball inside Alabama's 40-yard line. It was game on for the Crimson Tide's defense.

The first time, the Tide knocked out star quarterback Colt McCoy with a shoulder injury. The Longhorns nonetheless drove for a first-and-goal at Alabama's 1-yard line. Offsetting penalties put the ball at the 2, but two runs netted 1 yard and an incomplete pass brought on fourth down. The Longhorns settled for a field goal.

"To me, as a defense, we felt disrespect, because they tried to run the ball on us on the goal line," said Terrence Cody, the Tide's 354-pound senior All-American nose guard. "We're stubborn to give up touchdowns at the goal line. We feel like that's our house."

After an onsides kick, Texas had the ball at Alabama's 30-yard line, but the Longhorns were unable to get a first down and settled for three more points.

"When you give one of the best offenses the ball inside the 40-yard line and to hold them to two field goals, that says a lot about your defense," Tide linebacker Cory Reamer said.

After Alabama led 24-6 at halftime, Texas closed to 24-21 with 6:15 left in the game, but Alabama forced three turnovers the rest of the way and pulled away to a 37-21 victory. The key?

"We kept our cool," said junior middle linebacker Rolando McClain, who played despite battling a stomach bug.

And the Tide defense forced five turnovers overall.

Reamer said the early 6-0 deficit was nothing for the defense to worry about.

"We've been in worse situations," he said. "We got down real fast at Auburn, 14-0, and battled back."

Texas backup quarterback Garrett Gilbert had four passes intercepted.

The big one came at the end of the first half. On second-and-1 from the Longhorns' 37-yard line, he tried to throw a screen pass, but defensive end Brandon Deaderick tipped the ball. Defensive end Marcell Dareus caught it

Alabama defensive back Chris Rogers (1) (left) and Alabama defensive lineman Marcell Dareus (57) congratulate Alabama linebacker Eryk Anders (32) after his sack of Texas quarterback Garrett Gilbert (3) to clinch the victory. **STAFF PHOTO/MARK ALMOND**

and returned the interception 28 yards for a touchdown.

Gilbert threw two touchdown passes in the second half, but with 3:08 left in the game, he was sacked by Eryk Anders, who forced a fumble that Courtney Upshaw recovered at the Long-horns' 3-yard line. Three plays later, the Tide scored.

"He came out pretty shaky at first," Reamer said of Gilbert. "He got in a rhythm, and he got them in a position to win the game. We knew we had to step up."

Just For Kicks

Texas and Alabama take long strides to keep each other off balance

By MARK McCARTER

The least-likely passer, P.J. Fitzgerald, was aiming for the least-likely receiver, Dre' Kirkpatrick. Between the two, they have thrown and caught only one more pass for Alabama this season than you have.

It was a fake punt pass play born in a film room one day, though it seemed conceived in a backyard game of touch.

When Texas safety Blake Gideon sniffed out the play and made a leaping, stumbling interception on the Alabama 37 only moments into the BCS National Championship Game, it seemed that Alabama might have gotten too creative for its own good. Especially after Texas drove for a quick field goal.

"It was pretty much a miscommunication," said Fitzgerald, who rued the destruction of a perfect passer rating — 1-for-1 coming in.

"Me and Dre' weren't on the same page," he said. "It happens to any quarterback."

In the aftermath of Alabama's 37-21 victory, the play was little more than a footnote. Fitzgerald was able to laugh about it. Still, it led to Texas' first points.

By the same token, it was also emblematic of the influence of the kicking game all evening long, and a considerable bit of trickery on both sides.

It was a major weapon for Alabama, which was able to shift field position. Even if the Tide didn't score, it typically moved the ball with some effectiveness and at least kept Texas mired deep in its own land.

Texas was clearly worried about putting the ball into the hands of Javier Arenas and Alabama was skittish about Jordan Shipley.

"A return man can change the game in one play," Fitzgerald said.

"The two teams have great returners," Arenas said. "A game such as this, both guys, both teams have proven to come through in big situations. You try to eliminate that."

Texas' first-half kickoffs were sky kicks — "alternative kicks," Leigh Tiffin called them — with Justin Tucker booting the ball high but shallow, enabling defenders to arrive quicker on the scene.

It was a tradeoff: Good field position for Alabama against the gamble that Arenas might make it great field position.

It worked nicely on the second kick, which looked like a high pop fly dropping between two infielders and an outfielder. Baron Huber ran out from under it, Julio Jones — the most logical receiver — was blocked out of the way and Curtis Brown recovered for Texas. That set up the second Hunter Lawrence field goal.

Fitzgerald, who has been inconsistent in his attempts to plop kicks deep in enemy territory, had a masterpiece late in the second quarter that stuck Texas on its own 2 when Kirkpatrick made a scrambling dive to down the ball.

Texas was equally reluctant to let Arenas catch a punt, but he finally had a chance when the Longhorns failed to crawl from that deep hole. A short punt in the second quarter and his 12-yard runback led to, yes, still another kick — a 26-yard Tiffin field goal for a 17-6 lead.

When Texas finally scored a touchdown late in the third, it pulled an onside kick that it recovered at midfield. As was typical for the game, the Longhorns made little progress. They had to punt.

The success of Alabama's kick returner Javier Arenas (28), right was a major reason for Texas' elaborate kicking strategies.

Tide runs its way to a national title

DON KAUSLER JR.

This was the heavyweight matchup, the supreme battle that was supposed to settle the national championship.

An Alabama running game that featured the Heisman Trophy winner was matched against the nation's top rushing defense Thursday night.

And the outcome?

No contest.

It took the Crimson Tide a few minutes to warm up, but after it did, it ran over and around the Longhorns in a 37-21 victory for the national championship.

"We really wanted to run the ball," said right guard Barrett

Jones, a redshirt freshman. "We knew if we played assignment football and hit 'em in the mouth, no defense likes to be hit in the mouth."

Mark Ingram and Trent Richardson provided a 1-2 punch as the Tide ran 51 times for 205 yards against a defense that was allowing only 62.15 yards rushing per game.

"We room together," Ingram said of Richardson. "We said we were going to both gain 100 yards. We knew we needed to carry the team on our backs."

Ingram, the first Alabama player to win the 75-year-old Heisman Trophy, ran 22 times for 116 yards and two touchdowns. He sat out much of the third quarter with leg cramps but came back to run six times for 24 yards and a touchdown in the

Alabama running back Trent Richardson (3) gets outside of Texas defender Texas linebacker Roddrick Muckelroy (38).
STAFF PHOTO/ BUTCH DILL

fourth quarter.

Richardson, a freshman, ran 19 times for 109 yards, and he scored on a 49-yard run in a 24-point second quarter. The Tide ran for 148 yards in the first half.

"We just did what we've been doing all year," left tackle James Carpenter said.

Richardson ran for 41 yards in the fourth quarter.

"I thought we were going to have to run the ball against them," Richardson said. "Our line blocked well. Coach did some good play-calling."

His touchdown run on a second-and-10 play from the Texas 49-yard line gave the Tide a 14-6 lead midway through the second quarter.

"It was a counter play," he said. "We faked right, and I ran left. They all went the opposite way. I saw the hole and just went."

The hole was opened by center William Vlachos and left guard Mike Johnson. "It was pretty big," Richardson said.

Texas held the Tide to minus-6 yards rushing on eight attempts in the third quarter.

"I think we might have come out a little satisfied in the second half," Jones said. "We weren't hitting them as hard. But in the fourth quarter, when the game was on the line, that's been our thing: finishing."

Rising Star

Marcell Darius named defensive player of the game

By KEVIN SCARBINSKY

Write it down.

It's entirely possible, before his college career is done, that Alabama sophomore defensive end Marcell Dareus will eclipse senior nose guard Terrence Cody.

Not physically, of course.

Dareus stands 6-foot-4 and weighs 296 pounds.

Cody is listed at 6-5 and 354, and that's before breakfast.

It's not easy for the sun or the moon to cast a shadow over the enormously talented and popular Mount Cody.

But after sunset Thursday in the BCS Championship Game, it was Dareus, the second-year player from Huffman High School in Birmingham, who played like a star.

Who knocked Texas star Colt McCoy out of the game for good in the first quarter?

Dareus, with a clean, hard, backside hit on the quarterback's right shoulder, his throwing arm, as McCoy tried to turn an option keeper upfield.

"I really didn't want to hurt him," Dareus said. "Injuries are a part of the game."

At that moment, the Longhorns lost a senior leader who'd won more games as a starting quarterback than any other in major college history.

"I really have no pain in my arm," McCoy said afterward. "I just can't feel my arm. My arm is dead."

Who knocked Texas out of the game, seemingly for good, just before halftime?

Dareus, who snatched a bouncing ball off an ill-advised shovel pass for an interception. He ran it back 28 yards for a touchdown with three seconds left in the second quarter, with moves that had to make Mark Ingram smile.

That score gave Alabama a 24-6 halftime lead, from which Texas never recovered.

"My first reaction was to grab the ball," Dareus said. "After that, I blanked out."

Who was named defensive player of the game?

Not junior middle linebacker Rolando McClain, even though he overcame a stomach virus earlier in the week to lead the Alabama defense as usual.

Not senior cornerback Javier Arenas, who contributed two critical interceptions.

The defensive player of the game in the biggest game of the year was Dareus.

"I can't believe I got defensive MVP," he said.

He'd made an impact during the regular season, but in spots on a deep and experienced defensive line.

He played in all 13 games, but started only four.

He led the team in sacks, but his total of 6.5 ranked eighth in the SEC and tied for 73rd nationally.

He showed glimpses of great potential, but then came Thursday night, and his first career interception and his first career knockout of a two-time Heisman finalist.

"Marcell Dareus got the hit on (McCoy) that changed the game," Alabama coach Nick Saban said.

When the game was done, the sophomore won the award that may change his life.

Cody, the man mountain in the middle, is moving on.

Dareus, the difference-maker off the edge, is coming back and coming on.

"When I came out of Birmingham, I was a mediocre recruit," Dareus said. "I didn't think I was going to accomplish all this."

Alabama Marcell Dareus (57) breaks away from Texas quarterback Garrett Gilbert (3) for a touchdown after an interception.

STAFF PHOTO/ BILL STARLING

Alabama running back Mark Ingram (22) slides into the end zone after scoring a touchdown to clinch the win.

THE COACHES' TROPHY

Make no mistake, Saban is the real McCoy

By MARK McCARTER

Buy into the program if you're a player. Buy a big-money coach if you're the director of athletics.

Buy, if you'd like, a 3-by-3 inch chunk of freeze-dried Bermuda grass they'll be peeling off the Rose Bowl surface and preserving under glass as mementos.

Buy a whole bag full of national championship T-shirts and caps. Buy a bunch of new helmets to use as the Alabama logo. Gotta put 13 on the side now. The 12 championships of Tide history, are, well, history.

And preserve under glass this glorious night that began with breathtaking pageantry, with fireworks lighting up the blackberry skies over a bowl of crimson, white, houndstooth and burnt or-

ange, and ended with a blizzard of confetti showering a Gatorade-soaked Nick Saban, lifting a crystal football to the sky.

Preserve these words under glass:

Alabama 37, Texas 21.

Thirteen National Championships.

Fact is, at least from a national perspective, there will be something of an asterisk hung on this, and that won't be fair to Alabama.

The asterisk: What if quarterback Colt McCoy hadn't gotten hurt on the Longhorns' first series?

You'll be able to hear that topic debated today on talk radio until your ears bleed.

One thing is likely, Texas would have taken a 14-0 lead instead of a 6-0 lead.

Instead, things were left in the hands of redshirt freshman Garrett Gilbert. He was one of those high school players the recruiting gurus drool over, and he was clearly anointed The Next, once McCoy graduated. "Next" wasn't supposed to come Thursday, in the biggest game of the year.

Early, he looked shaky as a Chihuahua in a thunderstorm

Alabama Coach Nick Saban and
Alabama running back Mark
Ingram (22) smile after winning.

STAFF PHOTO/ MARK ALMOND

before passing Texas into contention in the second half.

Ultimately, though, it wasn't about who wasn't on the field.

It was about who was on the sidelines.

Nick Saban.

This game, and this season, was what everybody was wishing for when it rubbed a magic lamp three years and four days ago and Saban poofed out of it instead of a genie.

Winning games and winning conference and national championships may have been the mandate. They were the tangible goals, the W's on a scoreboard, the new chapters in Alabama history.

As much as anything, though, Saban's job was to restore luster to a tarnished program. Controversies, NCAA punishments, ill-advised or ill-fated coaching hires and just sheer underachievement turned Alabama into a mortal program.

It's not uncommon. Sport is cyclical. Look at the powerhouses that spiraled downward briefly only to return to greatness. Southern Cal. Oklahoma. Miami. And there's Notre Dame, still clutching its "help me and I've fallen and I can't get up" bracelet.

Alabama is the latest phoenix to soar from its own ashes.

"We jelled," said linebacker Corey Reamer. "We knew we were going to be something special."

Credit goes to Mal Moore, the director of athletics who stubbornly pursued Saban like a lovelorn teenager, and to Saban himself.

He may be prickly with the media and distant to the public. But — hardly a news flash — Saban can flat out coach and recruit.

He has convinced a bunch of kids of a generation where you can barely beg them to make their beds and use a napkin at dinner to buy into a process of hard work, focus and dedication. "They all bought into the things we needed to do," Saban said. "To work hard and dominate the opposition."

In three short seasons, Alabama became dominant again. Saban restored luster.

Not only did he put Alabama football back on the map, but on a night for the ages, when it snowed two inches of crimson and white in Southern California, Nick Saban put Alabama back in its customary spot in the football galaxy.

Alabama defender Mark Barron (4) tackles Texas receiver Malcolm Williams (9).

ABC a winner too

By JON SOLOMON

Good riddance, Fox. ABC demonstrated Thursday night why college football's national championship game finds itself in better hands with Walt Disney than Rupert Murdoch.

The BCS National Championship Game wasn't just Alabama's return to the pinnacle of college football. It was also ABC Sports/ESPN taking its rightful place back on the sport's center stage.

ABC's broadcast was attractive, detailed and informative. In a game that centered on Colt McCoy's injury on Texas' first possession, ABC was all over the story and explained what his departure meant.

"(Texas offensive coordinator) Greg Davis is calling plays with one hand behind his back," said analyst Kirk Herbstreit, who was on top of his game as usual.

It was as if viewers awoke from their four-year nightmare of Fox, whose run with the BCS ended this week after the Orange Bowl. Because the Rose Bowl has a separate TV deal from the rest of the BCS games, ABC aired Thursday night's broadcast as a jumpstart to next year's BCS games.

ESPN, which runs ABC Sports, paid $125 million for the rights to the Fiesta, Orange and Sugar bowls, as well as the BCS title games, from 2011 to 2014. ABC will still be the home of the Rose Bowl during that period.

My problem with Fox was its lack of credibility. The network doesn't air regular-season games, and it showed in the sport's biggest games.

Announcers spoke more generically than intimately about teams. Cameras treated every pause in action as license to air fan reaction from the crowd or band, regardless whether it was warranted.

Fox tried too hard to force a game-day environment onto television viewers who don't need that, not with HDTVs that give viewers at home a better picture than many fans at the game. Just the football, please.

ABC did that Thursday night. The only thing better would have been if Keith Jackson flipped the coin and returned to the booth in his prime to call the game.

I'm not a big fan of Brent Musburger, who overdramatizes moments far too often. I didn't understand why he was so stunned that Nick Saban accepted the ball after the opening coin toss. Alabama has taken the ball first before.

But Musburger was dead on with Alabama's bizarre fake punt on a fourth-and-23 from its 20-yard line to start the game. "Nick Saban goes way against his philosophy and goes with a (Bill) Belichick call," Musburger said, referring to Belichick's controversial fourth-down play against the Indianapolis Colts earlier this season.

Sideline reporter Lisa Salters provided timely updates on McCoy's injury. She talked to McCoy's father and got interesting information that McCoy wanted to return to the game, but his father, coach Mack Brown and the team doctor told him it wasn't worth the risk given his NFL future.

At halftime, Salters asked Brown the pointed question on everybody's mind: Why did he try to score in the final seconds before halftime deep in his own territory with a backup quarterback? A shovel pass by Gilbert was tipped and intercepted by Alabama for a touchdown.

"Well, the chance is about as safe as you've got," Brown told Salters. "It's an underneath shovel pass. It's like a draw. If it's not there, you throw it in the ground. We were trying to get past the 50 so we could take a deep shot."

ESPN analyst Lee Corso was incredulous at halftime about the decision.

"A bonehead call by the offensive staff," Corso shouted. "Who the hell goes for it with 15 seconds to go against the No. 1 defense in the world?"

As the game got closer, Herbstreit did a nice job pointing out how Gilbert was reading Alabama's defense better. And in the nice-timing department, right after Herbstreit noted Alabama hadn't sacked Texas all night, Eryk Anders iced the game with a sack that caused a fumble that the Crimson Tide recovered.

Alabama is back. More importantly for college football, so is ABC/ESPN.

Alabama running back Mark Ingram
(22) dives for extra yardage over Texas
defender Aaron Williams (4).

STAFF PHOTO/ BILL STARLING

Party on!

Tide fans loud and happy

By DAWN KENT

Alabama fans and students who gathered inside a bar on The Strip in Tuscaloosa on Thursday night wanted their team in Pasadena to hear them as the final seconds ticked off the clock at the BCS National Championship Game.

The screaming crowd in The Houndstooth then spilled outside, where T-shirts and hats proclaiming the school's latest football title were already on sale on the sidewalk.

Fireworks, blaring Lynyrd Skynyrd music and lots of hugs and hand slaps completed the scene on The Strip, which up to that point had been quiet as people were holed up around TVs on a chilly night.

There was a heavy Tuscaloosa police presence as the crowd and traffic began to build after the game.

Many fans in the area apparently had been watching the game in homes, as most popular bars and restaurants weren't full. The Northport Dreamland sold lots of takeout orders during the afternoon, and only a handful of diners were there an hour before gametime.

Alabama fans James Alley, Kate Jozefiak, both Tuscumbia, and Joshua Molton, Dothan, react as Mark Ingram scores late in the fourth quarter of the game as they watch the BCS National Championship game.

STAFF PHOTO/HAL YEAGER

The university's campus was mostly deserted earlier Thursday, as students' return from the holiday break was delayed because of the game.

About two hours before kickoff, some students watched pre-game programming on TVs scattered throughout the Ferguson Center.

A watch party was being held for students who had already returned — mostly freshmen who were there for orientation or international students.

More than 200 students had come through by 5:30 p.m. for free T-shirts and barbecue, said Shane Dorrill, a university spokes-man.

Paper palm fronds and Bama shakers decorated the tables, as game highlights played on multiple flat screens.

Many students, faculty and alumni made the trek to Pasadena, Dorrill said.

"We wanted to try to give those who are here a way to be a part of the game," he said.

Kathryn Cox and Kevin Adams, two students from Scottsboro, said they returned to campus early because of the game.

"We definitely wanted to celebrate here," Cox said.

How They Scored

FIRST QUARTER

TEXAS—Hunter Lawrence 18 FG. Key plays: Alabama held the Longhorns to a field goal after facing a first-and-goal at the 1. But the biggest event in the drive was Texas quarterback Colt McCoy leaving the game with a shoulder injury. D.J. Monroe ran 10 yards to the 1 for Texas, stopped by Tide safety Mark Barron. Drive: 10 plays, 36 yards in 3:50. Texas 3, Alabama 0. (9:11 remaining).

TEXAS—Lawrence 42 FG. Key plays: Alabama busted the coverage on a short kickoff, failing to field the ball as it landed in front of deep returner Julio Jones, giving Texas essentially a deep onside kick recovery. But with McCoy still on the bench, the Longhorns couldn't move the ball and settled for Lawrence's second field goal. Drive: 4 plays, 5 yards in 1:07. Texas 6, Alabama 0. (8:04).

SECOND QUARTER

ALABAMA—Mark Ingram 2 run (Leigh Tiffin kick). Key plays: The Tide steadied itself behind its bruising running game. Ingram ran for eight yards on the first play, then nine more on the next. Greg McElroy completed a 22-yard pass to Julio Jones on a deep out along the left sideline. Then Ingram charged nine yards up the middle and, two plays later, scored from the 2 while running behind defensive tackle-turned-fullback Terrence Cody to give Alabama its first lead. Drive: 7 plays, 57 yards in 3:27. Alabama 7, Texas 6. (14:18).

ALABAMA—Trent Richardson 49 run (Tiffin kick), 7:59. Key plays: On second-and-10, Richardson blasted up the middle on a delayed handoff and the Longhorns never touched him. All-American Mike Johnson sealed off the gaping hole with a pancake block as Alabama's' running game continued to dominate. Drive: 2 plays, 49 yards in 0:45. Alabama 14, Texas 6. (7:59).

ALABAMA—Tiffin 26 FG. Key plays: Alabama failed to capitalize on superb field position, settling for the field goal after taking over at the Longhorn 29 following a short punt and a 12-yard return by Javier Arenas. Tide coach Nick Saban also took a conservative approach on the drive, opting for a field goal on fourth-and-1 at the Texas 9. Ingram ran for 13 yards to push the Tide inside the 10. Drive: 6 plays, 20 yards in 1:51. Alabama 17, Texas 6. (0:29).

ALABAMA—Marcell Dareus 28 interception return (Tiffin kick). Key plays: Instead of simply running out the clock, Texas opted to attempt a shovel pass to D.J. Monroe on second-and-1. But a surge from the Alabama defensive front led to the ball being juggled and Dareus snatched it. He broke two tackles en route to his rumbling touchdown run. Alabama 24, Texas 6. (0:03).

THIRD QUARTER

TEXAS—Jordan Shipley 44 pass from Garrett Gilbert (Lawrence kick). Key plays: The slumbering Texas offense dropped a bolt of lightning on Alabama. Gilbert made his best throw of the night on a deep post pattern to Shipley that beat Alabama cornerback Javier Arenas. The TD pass was set up by a short screen pass to the right to Marquise Goodwin that gained 13 yards on third-and-8 for a first down at the Tide 44. Gilbert had just 60 yards passing before the TD pass. Drive: 5 plays, 59 yards in 1:44. Alabama 24, Texas 13. (1:31).

FOURTH QUARTER

TEXAS—Shipley 28 pass from Gilbert (Dan Buckner pass from Gilbert). Key plays: Gilbert began to blossom by hitting a series of passes that brought the Longhorns within striking distance. Alabama blew the coverage on the touchdown, leaving Shipley wide open down the right sideline. Gilbert picked apart the Tide secondary on the drive, completing 7-of-8 passes for 64 of the 65 yards on the drive. Gilbert primarily hit Alabama with short passes underneath the defense to Shipley, who caught five passes on the drive. Drive: 9 plays, 65 yards in 4:58. Alabama 24, Texas 21. (6:15).

ALABAMA—Ingram 1 run (Tiffin kick). Key plays: Alabama clinched the championship with a huge play on defense. Blitzing linebacker Eryk Anders hit Gilbert from the blind side, causing a fumble that linebacker Courtney Upshaw recovered at the 3. Three 1-yard runs by Ingram delivered the touchdown. It was the first quarterback sack of the night for the defense and Ingram's second touchdown in a game where he rushed for 116 yards on 22 carries. Drive: 3 plays, 3 yards in 1:01. Alabama 31, Texas 21. (2:01).

ALABAMA—Richardson 2 run (kick failed). Key plays: One final moment of joy before the celebration came when Javier Arenas intercepted his second pass of the game, setting up Richardson's second touchdown. Richardson gained 17 yards on first down and a facemask penalty on Texas put the ball at the Longhorn 5. And as soon as Richardson dove into the end zone, Saban received the celebratory dumping of the Gatorade. Drive: 3 plays, 27 yards in 1:01. Alabama 37, Texas 21. (0:47).

Alabama's Dre Kirkpatrick (21) celebrates
after a stop against Texas.

STAFF PHOTO/ BILL STARLING

sec champi
florida

onship game

CRIMSON TIDE	32
GATORS	13

12.05.09 | 3 p.m. | Georgia Dome | Atlanta, GA

Mark of a Champ

Ingram runs Crimson Tide past Gators in SEC title game

By GENTRY ESTES

Alabama wide receiver Darius Hanks had his own eye patches ready for Saturday night.

One read "NO," the other, "REGRETS."

"In the back of our heads, it was always Florida," Hanks said. "We wanted this game since last year, when we lost. We came out, and we got our vengeance."

And it wasn't close.

With a style and swagger that fit the enormous occasion and the words under Hanks' eyes, No. 2-ranked Alabama left nothing on the field and no doubt. A 32-13 pounding of the No. 1 Gators in Saturday's SEC championship game ended with the Crimson Tide taking a knee, coach Nick Saban chest-bumping tailback Mark Ingram, and tears falling down Florida quarterback Tim Tebow's cheeks.

The crimson celebration had just started. It's probably still rolling, just like the team that will now play for the program's 13th national championship.

Though Alabama secured its first SEC title since 1999, the big treat won by drubbing the Gators is the same one Florida took from the Georgia Dome last year: A spot in the BCS national title game, with Texas the expected opponent, to be held Jan. 7 in the Rose Bowl in Pasadena, Calif.

A year of frustration for the Crimson Tide played out in 60 minutes and a much-anticipated game that was far more lopsided than anyone could have expected.

"A lot in life comes down to expectations sometimes," Saban said, "and we didn't come here looking for a moral victory. ...This team wanted to prove that they could do something special."

Alabama (13-0) controlled both lines of scrimmage and scored on its first two possessions Saturday, never trailing in front of 77,514 fans. Ingram won this battle of Heisman Trophy candidates with Tebow by rushing for 113 yards and three touchdowns.

"Ever since last year, when we walked off the field (in Atlanta), everything we did was to beat Florida," Ingram said. "Everything we did was to be better than Florida. We felt like coming in that they didn't respect us. ... We weren't going to be stopped. There wasn't anything that was going to keep us from winning this game."

Perhaps most surprisingly, Alabama junior Greg McElroy won the battle of the quarterbacks, earning the game's Most Valuable Player honors by throwing for 239 yards on 12-of-18 passing.

"The breakout performance wasn't mine," McElroy said. "It was my offensive line. It was my wide receivers. It was Mark, Trent (Richard-

Alabama running back Mark Ingram (22) breaks away fron Florida defensive tackle Troy Epps (98).

STAFF PHOTO/ MARK ALMOND

ap top 10 released 12.06.09

TEAM	1ST	2ND	3RD	4TH	FINAL
ALABAMA	9	10	7	6	32
FLORIDA	3	10	0	0	13

Attendance   75,514 Georgia Dome

SCORING SUMMARY

UA L Tiffin 48 yd field goal, 9 plays, 47 yds, TOP 4:23
UA M Ingram 7 yd run (L Tiffin kick failed), 8 plays, 76 yds, TOP 3:56
UF C Sturgis 48 yd field goal, 12 plays, 56 yds, TOP 5:05
UA L Tiffin 34 yd field goal, 12 plays, 68 yds, TOP 5:47
UF D Nelson 23 yd pass from T Tebow (C Sturgis kick), 4 plays, 70 yds, TOP 1:32
UA M Ingram 3 yd run (L Tiffin kick), 2 plays, 72 yds, TOP 0:59
UF C Sturgis 32 yd field goal, 5 plays, 65 yds, TOP 2:14
UA C Peek 17 yd pass from G McElroy (L Tiffin kick), 5 plays, 74 yds, TOP 2:48
UA M Ingram 1 yd run (G McElroy pass failed), 17 plays, 88 yds, TOP 8:47

TEAM STATISTICS

	UA	UF
FIRST DOWNS	26	13
NET YARDS RUSHING	251	88
NET YARDS PASSING	239	247
COMPLETIONS-ATTEMPTS-INT	12-18-0	20-35-1
TOTAL OFFENSE YARDS	490	335
PENALTIES: NUMBER-YARDS	1-5	5-57
PUNTS-YARDS	2-83	4-195
PUNT RETURNS: NUMBER-YDS-TD	1-8-0	1-12-0
KICKOFF RETURNS: NUMBER-YDS-TD	3-79-0	6-161-0
POSSESSION TIME	39:37	20:23
SACKS BY: NUMBER-YARDS LOST	0-0	1-10
FIELD GOALS	2-2	2-2
FUMBLES: NUMBER-LOST	1-0	0-0

INDIVIDUAL OFFENSIVE STATISTICS

RUSHING: UA – M Ingram 28-113; T Richardson 11-80; R Upchurch 7-57;
              G McElroy 4-10
              UF – T Tebow 10-63; J Demps 1-9; B James 1-9; C Rainey 2-7
PASSING: UA – G McElroy 18-12-0, 239
              UF – T Tebow 35-20-1, 247
RECEIVING: UA – M Maze 5-96; C Peek 3-39; M Ingram 2-76 J Jones 2-28
              UF – A Hernandez 8-85; D Nelson 4-53; R Cooper 3-77;
              D Thompson 2-22; B James 1-9; O Hines 1-4

INDIVIDUAL DEFENSIVE STATISTICS

INTERCEPTIONS: UA – Javier Arenas 1-0   UF – None
SACKS: UA – None   UF – A. Black 1
TACKLES: UA – M Barron 4-3; K Jackson 3-3; R McClain 3-2; C Reamer 3-1;
              R Green 2-1
              UF – J Howard 8-2; B Spikes 4-5; A Black 7-1; M Wright 7-0; B Hicks 4-2;
              R Stamper 3-2; D Doe 2-3

1	2	3	4	5	6	7	8	9	10
ALABAMA	TEXAS	TCU	CINCINNATI	FLORIDA	BOISE STATE	OREGON	OHIO STATE	GEORGIA TECH	IOWA

Alabama running back Roy Upchurch (5) celebrates!

STAFF PHOTO/ MARK ALMOND

son), Roy (Upchurch). It was the defense. In order to be a championship team, coach tells us, you have to have a team full of champions. ... This team can now call themselves champions."

The most telling sign of the Crimson Tide's dominance on both lines was that it nearly doubled Florida in possession time, totaling 39:37 to the Gators' 20:23. McElroy orchestrated three drives of at least 12 plays, including a 17-play, 88-yard monster of a touchdown march that killed 8:47 off the clock and bled into the start of the fourth quarter. When Ingram scored on a 1-yard run to cap the march, the lead hit 19 points and the Gators had 13:49 to get it back.

Florida's realistic comeback hopes died when Alabama cornerback Javier Arenas intercepted Tebow in the end zone, sending Gators fans into the cold evening.

"We're kind of in a territory we haven't been in a while," UF coach Urban Meyer said. "You're not going to win every game you play."

But this game that meant so much for the future of this Alabama season actually goes all the way back to the most painful moment of the previous season. The Gators scored two unanswered touchdowns in the final quarter to rally for a 31-20 victory in last season's SEC championship game en route to their own national title. The Crimson Tide never forgot, using it as motivation during the offseason. Preparation among coaches began almost one year ago exactly.

Before offseason workouts began in February, Saban showed pictures of the SEC championship game and told players that before anything else, "we had to work to beat the best team in our league."

"That's all we talked about," Alabama linebacker Rolando McClain said. "We knew we had a long season ahead of us, but we always had this game in the back of our mind. I mean, it just drove us."

The Crimson Tide's game plan allowed the offense to roll to a whopping 490 yards against a defense that entered Saturday as the nation's best. It also kept Tebow from ever getting comfortable, and although he wound up throwing for 247 yards, Alabama successfully kept him in the pocket, which was the plan. Tebow rushed for 63 yards. But no other Florida players topped 9 yards, and the former Heisman winner ended his final SEC game in tears on the Gators' bench.

"It was frustrating, obviously," Tebow said. "This is not how we wanted to finish our season in the SEC. There were a lot of goals we won't be able to accomplish.... Coming in we felt like we were prepared. But obviously, we could have done a better job."

Alabama celebrated on the Georgia Dome turf as a team, climbing onto the podium to receive the SEC title trophy before delirious fans.

"Does it get any better than this?" right guard Barrett Jones said amid the cheers. "You've got to play your best game of the year, and I feel like we did."

"When you're little, you used to play the video games and you want that perfect team," freshman linebacker Nico Johnson said, "And I'm playing for one right now that won the SEC championship and (is) going to the national championship."

The Crimson Tide's assistant coaches quietly received handshakes from well-wishers, their own form of celebration in the aftermath. Players were issued roses in the locker room, taking pictures among each other. And, of course, a few began talking about Pasadena.

"We've got one more to finish it off," senior linebacker Cory Reamer said. "It's beyond my wildest dreams to be a part of something like this. This university has been through a lot in the last decade, and I'm just glad I'm still here.

"It's been a long time coming."

Alabama defensive back Marquis Johnson (24) breaks up a pass intended for Florida's Jeffery Demps (2) in the second quarter.

STAFF PHOTO/ HAL YEAGER

Alabama running back Mark Ingram (22) runs as Alabama offensive lineman William Vlachos (73) blocks a Florida defender.

STAFF PHOTO/ MARK ALMOND

Ingram returns to Heisman-like self vs. Gators

By BILL BRYANT

Mark Ingram stood patiently in front of the camera that would broadcast his face and words across the nation, while all around him bedlam was in full effect after Alabama's 32-13 win Saturday over Florida in the SEC Championship game.

The sophomore tailback chatted cheerfully with teammate Justin Woodall, a rose in his hand signifying Pasadena and all that it will offer next month.

"You're going live, baby," Woodall said gleefully.

During the final moments before the return from commercial break, Ingram leaned in and whispered something into the senior safety's ear.

"Go have fun," Ingram said, pointing to the stage on the Georgia Dome turf, where the majority of their teammates were celebrating under a deluge of confetti.

Ingram had already had a very good time. Good enough to earn a trip to New York in the near future? Close to absolutely.

Good enough to walk those final few yards to wrap his arms around the Heisman Trophy? Well, after appearing to fall off the cliff last week against Auburn like Wile E. Coyote did so often while chasing the road runner, there's still a chance.

Facing the nation's No. 1 defense, Ingram rushed for 113 yards, caught two passes for another 76 - including a 69-yarder on a simple dump-off - and scored three touchdowns. In the process, he also broke the school record for rushing yardage (Ingram now has 1,542 yards to Bobby Humphrey's 1,471 in 1986).

"We came out here as a team and fought. We weren't going to be denied tonight," said Ingram, coming off a 30-yard effort and a hip pointer last week against Auburn. "Right now I just want to enjoy this victory. We'll wait for (the Heisman announcement) next week."

Ingram didn't bust any runs of major significance - his long was 15 yards - but he did get more than his share of 5-, 6- and 7-yarders that have come to personify this offense over the past two seasons.

"If he's not the Heisman winner there must be somebody out there with a lot of talent," left guard Mike Johnson said. "He's got a lot of heart. For such a young kid, he's got such grace. You couldn't ask to block for a better guy."

The 69-yard pass play, which came after about a 5-yard throw from quarterback Greg McElroy, went a long way toward answering a Florida score that cut the Crimson Tide's lead to 12-10. Ingram scored on the next play from the 3.

"I think Mark showed a lot of resolve because he did have a hip pointer," Alabama coach Nick Saban said. "We didn't know how he would respond after last week's game where he got a little frustrated. But he went for it today (and) played a great game."

TEBOW: 'It was frustrating'

By DOUG SEGERST

Tears overflowing, Tim Tebow stood alone at midfield, surrounded by dozens of reporters.

His Florida teammates had left the field already. His state trooper escort hadn't, and as cameras clicked and reporters swarmed around him, Tebow stood in the makeshift pocket and waited.

For Nick Saban.

"I just wanted to tell him congratulations," explained Tebow, who greeted the man whose defense befuddled his team for most of the night, extending a handshake that was returned with an embrace.

And thus the torch was passed. The king is dead.

Long live the new SEC king.

Florida receiver David Nelson realized Florida's 22-game winning streak and national championship reign was in serious trouble at the end of the fourth quarter.

With Alabama leading 26-13, the

STAFF PHOTO/HAL YEAGER

Crimson Tide players turned to the fans with four fingers aloft while a weary Florida defense trudged silently to the sideline for a 90-second respite.

"I saw them holding up fingers, like they were going to dominate the fourth quarter," Nelson said. "Last year, we stuck it to them in the fourth quarter. This year, they wouldn't be denied."

Florida entered the game with the nation's No. 1 defense, one that was ravaged for 490 yards. Even by the end of the third quarter, Alabama had more yards (403) than the Gators had surrendered in a game this year. It was a defense that had to deal with the loss of its best player - defensive end Carlos Dunlap, who was suspended after being charged with a DUI early Tuesday morning.

"It's frustrating," said cornerback Joe Haden. "You know we have a good defense and we can't get off the field.

"There was nothing about distractions. It was about Alabama coming out and wanting this."

Haden said the Tide didn't show a single new wrinkle. Why? Because Alabama didn't have to.

"They ran the same things we've seen on video," he said. "We just weren't tackling. They'd bounce off the first person and we missed too many tackles."

Florida trailed 19-13 at halftime. In the fourth quarter, down 32-13 after an early Alabama touchdown and a fiery Tebow pep talk on the sideline, the Gators mounted two drives.

The first reached the Alabama 6 and ended in the end zone with a Javier Arenas interception. Four minutes later, a second threat ended at the Bama 13 on downs.

"It was frustrating. To say it wasn't, it would be a lie," Tebow said.

"We just played bad," said linebacker Ryan Stamper. "They beat us all across the board - offense, defense, you name it."

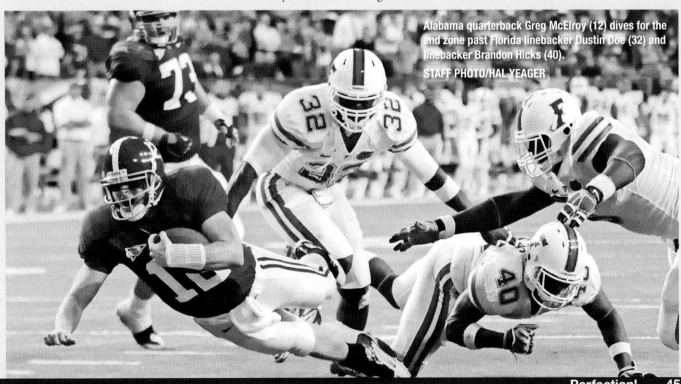

Alabama quarterback Greg McElroy (12) dives for the end zone past Florida linebacker Dustin Doe (32) and linebacker Brandon Hicks (40).
STAFF PHOTO/HAL YEAGER

Alabama quarterback Greg McElroy (12).

STAFF PHOTO/BILL STARLING

Promised and Delivered

With a new resolve, McElroy outshines Tebow

By JON SOLOMON

Superman wore a different-colored cape Saturday. Greg McElroy "out-Tebowed" Tim Tebow. Need a midseason promise? McElroy delivered on his. Need a remarkably efficient passing game? McElroy did it. Need some nifty runs? McElroy produced them. Need some emotion? McElroy posed like a pro wrestler.

"You leave here and wonder who was the Heisman winner, which quarterback?" Alabama offensive lineman Mike Johnson said.

From midseason criticism to SEC Championship Game MVP, McElroy delivered his best performance when it mattered most.

McElroy completed 12 of 18 passes for 239 yards against the nation's top-ranked defense in a 32-13 romp over Florida.

Only six weeks ago, McElroy stood in front of reporters after a 92-yard, two-interception performance against South Carolina and spoke of trying to regain his confidence. It was Alabama's version of the Tebow promise, the legendary speech Florida's quarterback gave after a 2008 loss to Ole Miss that propelled the Gators to the national title.

"But we'll get it figured out. I promise," McElroy said Oct. 17. "I promised my fans and promised the coaches and promised to the players that I will get it figured it out and we will get it straightened out. . . . I don't care if I spend every second and sleep in the football complex. I will do that to figure this thing out."

Wide receiver Marquis Maze said McElroy changed after the South Carolina game and reached a new level of leadership this week.

"He was in everybody's ear," said Maze, who caught five passes for 96 yards. "If somebody wasn't hustling, he'd get on them. Everybody gives Tebow all the glory, but there's other quarterbacks out there like Greg McElroy."

Running back Roy Upchurch said McElroy spoke up in practice all week, a rarity by him.

"He was giving more than he really has," Upchurch said. "I think that was the difference in this game, his preparation. That's probably the best I've seen him play."

This wasn't the rattled McElroy who locked in on Julio Jones too much against Ole Miss. This wasn't the care-taker McElroy who did just enough to win late in the season. This was McElroy letting it all hang out without making foolish plays.

"He did show a lot of poise for a first-year quarterback," Florida coach Urban Meyer said. "You saw it coming. You saw it last week against Auburn. And those things usually accelerate a quarterback's progress."

When Trent Richardson bounced outside for a second-quarter run, McElroy threw his body at Florida linebacker Brandon Hicks for a block. McElroy turned to the Florida bench and flexed his muscles, a move that McElroy said was by accident if it happened.

"This is a tremendous atmosphere, and I couldn't help but get overwhelmed by it at times," McElroy said.

The quarterback teammates dub "Vanilla Vick" used his feet too. McElroy picked up a first down by somehow tip-toeing down the sideline on a third-and-5, and later eluded a sack near the Florida goal line and somehow turned it into a near-touchdown.

"Greg all year has stepped up when we needed him most," offensive lineman Barrett Jones said. "We're so proud of the way he stepped up tonight and put it on his shoulders and said 'if you give me time, I'm going to find somebody.'"

McElroy now finds himself in a new place - Alabama lore.

Saban Wouldn't Sleep Till He Solved Florida Problem

By KEVIN SCARBINSKY

Nick Saban had confetti in his hair, but he had that faraway look on his face. Terry Saban could see it.

Her husband was standing on the podium after beating Florida 32-13 in the SEC Championship Game, after rewriting the ending to the Tim Tebow Story, chapter and verse.

Oh, the Alabama coach was smiling after banishing the demons that haunted him since the 2008 SEC Championship Game went the other way, but his wife knew what he was thinking.

Game over. Mission accomplished. Who's next?

"I could see it in his eyes when he was up on the stand with the trophy," Terry Saban said. "He's already, in his mind, planning for the next one. That's what he does, and that's what he loves."

In that case, Saban has to love his third Alabama football team, and not just because it created a space problem in the school's trophy case.

Alabama did win the school's first SEC championship in 10 years. Alabama will play for the school's first national title in 17 years in the Rose Bowl, which is fight-song music to a Tide fan's ears.

Alabama did its damage early and often Saturday, physically and forcefully, much like the 1992 team did against another Sunshine State champion, Miami, to win it all.

But Saban has to love this team because, like a dog that comes to resemble its owner, this team plays like its coach coaches.

It doesn't rest. It doesn't stop. It doesn't let go.

Alabama quarterback Greg McElroy (12) defensive coordinator Kirby Smart and Nick Saban react to a big defensive play in the fourth quarter.
STAFF PHOTO/HAL YEAGER

It took 365 days to solve the Florida problem, but Alabama did it with a vengeance. Alabama did more than lead from the first series to the final whistle.

Alabama made Tebow cry.

The cameras caught those tears and flashed them on the big-screens in the end zones, and the Alabama fans reveled in it.

The Alabama players? They expected it.

"Ever since last year when we walked off that field," running back Mark Ingram said, "everything we did, we did to beat Florida."

Witness Ingram limping after the game but not during his 69-yard sprint with a screen to answer Florida's first touchdown.

Watch Trent Richardson break tackles in the backfield to turn a 2-yard loss into a 7-yard gain.

See Greg McElroy, the game's MVP, the best quarterback on the field, make a block on that run, and did you see the quarterback flash a muscle pose at the Florida bench after the block?

"I don't have a lot to show off, so no," McElroy said. "And if I did so, it was totally by accident."

His game-long enthusiasm was no mistake.

"This game was full of emotion," he said. "It was a revenge game."

An SEC coach had told me to do the math, and it resulted in the stat of the week. Since he got to the league, Saban was 13-1 in revenge games.

Make that 14-1.

This is what happens when Saban gets enough of his players - "a critical mass," he said - to buy what he sells and think like he thinks.

Sooner or later, his school starts selling championship T-shirts.

It took Saban and his "organization," as he likes to call it, three years of grinding to solve Alabama's championship problem. Will he stop for a second to enjoy the moment?

"He says he'll celebrate for 24 hours, but what that really means is he's just gonna try to get a little sleep," his wife said. "He hasn't had much sleep recently.

"In between snoozes, I guarantee you, he's going to start X's and O's for the next one."

The process is almost complete, except for one thing.

The process is never complete.

That's what sets it, and the man who swears by it, apart.

mark

Making His Mark

Ingram gives Tide fans reason to care, cheer

By KEVIN SCARBINSKY

The biggest myth in Alabama football history used to be Forrest Gump.

And then Mark Ingram ran from Atlanta to Atlanta and didn't stop until he reached New York. The sophomore steadily and single-handedly shattered a bigger myth.

You know the one.

It says Alabama doesn't care about the Heisman Trophy.

It says Alabama cares only about national championships.

Alabama is 60 minutes away from another national title, but it turns out that the fan base is able to multi-task.

Judging by the messageboard hit lists of Southern electors who left Ingram off their ballots completely, and the talk-radio torching of one particular voter in this state who marked him second behind teammate Rolando McClain - gulp! - the Crimson Nation really does care about the Heisman.

But only when it has a player with a real chance to win one.

Ingram made the most of that chance Saturday night.

He made history as a classy winner of Alabama's first Heisman.

Ingram joined a proud, elite and exclusive fraternity from this state, alongside former Auburn quarterback Pat Sullivan, the 1971 Heisman winner, and former Auburn running back Bo Jackson, the 1985 winner.

Ingram (1,542 rushing yards in 13 games) didn't put up the same monster numbers as Jackson (1,786 yards in 11 games), but Ingram wasn't competing against Jackson.

And don't let anyone tell you Alabama's first bronze statue is tarnished because Ingram won by a mere 28 points, the tightest margin ever.

Until Saturday, the closest call in Heisman history came in 1985. Jackson nipped a forgettable Iowa quarterback named Chuck Long by a mere 45 points.

Close doesn't count, in Iron Bowls or Heisman totals. Walk away with the trophy, and you walk out with your head held high.

Now that Ingram has broken Alabama's Heisman drought, and Alabama fans have ended their Heisman apathy, it'll be up to the Alabama team to snap the Heisman jinx. That's the one that

ingram > Heisman Winner

Alabama running back Mark Ingram (22) pushes off South Carolina strong safety Darian Stewart (24) in the fourth quarter.

STAFF PHOTO/MARK ALMOND

seems to doom the Heisman winner if he happens to play for the national championship.

Alabama should know this one by heart because it got into the head of Miami quarterback, and Heisman winner, Gino Torretta, in the 1993 Sugar Bowl.

Consider a more current list of Heisman honorees who won the battle for the statue but, a month or so later, lost the national championship war.

> 2000: Florida State quarterback Chris Weinke. Lost the Orange Bowl to Oklahoma.

> 2001: Nebraska quarterback Eric Crouch. Lost the Rose Bowl to Miami.

> 2003: Oklahoma quarterback Jason White. Lost the Sugar Bowl to Nick Saban and LSU.

> 2005: USC running back Reggie Bush. Lost the Rose Bowl to Texas.

> 2006: Ohio State quarterback Troy Smith. Lost the BCS Championship Game to Florida.

> 2008: Oklahoma quarterback Sam Bradford. Lost the BCS title tilt to Florida.

Who was the most recent Heisman winner to add a national championship ring in a matter of weeks? USC quarterback Matt Leinart in 2004. He had the good fortune to face undeserving Oklahoma for the title rather than underrated Auburn.

So Ingram, while making history Saturday, will fight another kind of history Jan. 7 in Pasadena.

No doubt Will Muschamp and his Texas defense already had a target painted on Ingram's back.

That target just grew three sizes.

Ingram became the third straight sophomore to win the Heisman, following Tim Tebow and Bradford. Before Tebow, no sophomore had won it.

Somewhere, Trent Richardson is smiling at that streak. He'll be a sophomore next year.

Of course, as good as he is, he'll be no better than option 1B in Alabama's running back rotation.

Ingram's coming back, and he's bringing something with him. That precious stiff-arm statue.

It won't be the last statue this program sees this season.

Alabama running back Mark Ingram (22) carries the ball during the first half of their game against North Texas.

STAFF PHOTO/BILL STARLING

Ingram's Heisman Chances Hit Bump At Auburn

By JON SOLOMON

Mark Ingram's Heisman Trophy chances - and his health - took a major hit when he was held to a season-low 30 yards rushing in Alabama's 26-21 victory Friday.

Ingram didn't finish the game due to what coach Nick Saban described as a hip pointer.

Ingram left on the game-winning fourth-quarter drive. Once Ingram departed, freshman Trent Richardson caught a 17-yard pass and ran twice for seven yards, and senior Roy Upchurch won the game with a 4-yard touchdown catch.

Ingram said he was hurt after catching a screen pass earlier on that drive and having a helmet hit his hip area. Ingram said he left for good after a 1-yard run later in the drive because he tried to cut "but it wasn't happening."

The star sophomore is "bruised a little bit, but I'll be all right," he said.

The finish underscored a rough afternoon for Ingram, who many experts tabbed as the No. 1 Heisman candidate entering the game. Ingram had been averaging 127.2 rushing yards per game, fifth in the country.

Auburn's approach: Be physical, all day.

"We knew they were going to come in and pound the ball," Auburn defensive end Antonio Coleman said. "We stepped up to the challenge."

Auburn running back Ben Tate helped set the challenge two weeks ago by saying he believes he is the best running back in the state. Neither of the two 100-yard-a-game rushers cracked 50 or had a run longer than 11 yards.

If you were scoring at home Friday, the running back rushing lines read Richardson 51, Tate 45, Ingram 30.

"I support Ben Tate in whatever he says because he's a great running back," Coleman said. "After the game I walked up and told him he's a great running back. I'm not going to get into words on who's the best running back in the state. I'm just happy we held Mark Ingram, Heisman hopeful, to what, 22 yards? Thirty yards?"

Auburn entered Friday as the 88th-ranked rush defense at 169.7 yards per game. Alabama was held to 73 yards on 35 rush attempts, its lowest rushing total since gaining 31 in last season's Sugar Bowl loss to Utah.

Alabama's longest run was 8 yards. Offensive lineman Mike Johnson described Auburn's front as constantly moving before the snap and disguising blitzes. "It was obvious they got stuff off film and studied it well," Johnson said. "They were well-prepared."

Said Saban: "We probably weren't as prepared for it as we should have been."

Ingram said he doesn't care about the Heisman, which no Alabama player has ever won.

"For all the All-Americans to come in here, it's kind of surprising there's never been a Heisman winner," Ingram said. "But it's all about team, and it's all about the tradition here. The most ultimate goal for any team is to win the national championship, to win an SEC championship, to win any championship as a team. If we keep winning and we keep performing, everything else will take care of itself."

Alabama running back Mark Ingram (22) breaks away from Florida at the Georgia Dome.
STAFF PHOTO/MARK ALMOND

Running Wild

Alabama star Ingram gaining Heisman consideration

By GENTRY ESTES

Alabama's Mark Ingram is focused on the future, even as the past three weeks have changed seemingly everything around the sophomore tailback.

"People are excited for me," Ingram said. "It obviously makes you feel good, but you've got to keep moving forward, look ahead and not backwards."

The roulette wheel that is this year's Heisman Trophy race landed on Ingram this week, courtesy of a 246-yard rushing effort against South Carolina on national television. It was Ingram's third consecutive 100-yard game — bringing him to 905 rushing yards through seven games, numbers enhanced by the fact that the Crimson Tide is 7-0 and ranked No. 1 in the AP poll.

He's not only being tabbed as a candidate now, but a possible frontrunner. ESPN's poll of 15 experts for its "Heisman Watch" had Ingram No. 1 this week. He was barely ahead of Florida

quarterback Tim Tebow. Notre Dame quarterback Jimmy Clausen was third.

"It's an honor to be considered as one of the top candidates for that award, but I'm not too worried about it," Ingram said. "I'm just really worried about helping this team win and getting better every day as a player and just helping us win. If we just keep winning and I keep performing, everything else will take care of itself."

Ingram rolled through South Carolina despite hurting his knee early in the game. He said he was in pain, but fought through it by keeping it loose with exercises on the sideline. The soreness was worse than normal Sunday.

Despite analysts singing his praises, Ingram said he didn't watch much TV. He spent more time in ice to dull soreness and watching film of Tennessee, Saturday's 2:30 p.m. opponent in Tuscaloosa.

Asked how Ingram would handle the Heisman buzz, Crimson Tide coach Nick Saban replied, "He usually handles it pretty well."

"He had a lot of success doing things the way (he does) them,"

Alabama running back Mark Ingram (22) dives to score a touchdown in front of Florida safety Major Wright (21) in the first quarter of the SEC Championship Game.

STAFF PHOTO/MARK ALMOND

Saban said. "The best way to continue to have success is to remember what got you there and continue to do those things."

"It takes a special player to be able to handle a lot of praise, and Mark is one of those guys that although he can go out and have a great game, he can still find the negatives in the game and try to get those things corrected," quarterback Greg McElroy said.

As if on cue, Ingram said he has noticed the increased attention, but he says it's not consuming him.

"I really don't find any pressure," Ingram said. "I'm not worried about it. ... Everybody else thinks it is pressure, but around here, they kind of take the pressure off you a little bit."

If there is to be a Heisman Trophy campaign for Ingram, it will be waged on the field and not in a public relations war room. There are no current plans at UA to bombard voters with material — as has been done at other schools with mixed results — about Ingram, linebacker Rolando McClain, quarterback Greg McElroy or any other player who has been linked with Heisman speculation.

Such thinking fits in with Saban's philosophy.

"Coach Saban always emphasizes it's about the team and everybody jelling together so we can have great chemistry," Ingram said. "When we have a great team, the more awards people win anyway. I think it's more important to be a part of a great team and accomplish team awards, like winning a national or an SEC championship."

Championships? Alabama has a few of those. What it doesn't have is a Heisman Trophy to display on the glitzy upstairs wall of the football complex.

A campaign would also be uncharted territory for Saban. As a college head coach, Saban has never had one of his players finish in the top 10 of the voting for the Heisman.

Is Ingram the guy to change all that?

Tennessee might think so. The Vols have spent early moments of practice this week with additional, physical tackling drills with the Crimson Tide's No. 22 in mind.

"If we let Mark Ingram get started," UT defensive end Wes Brown said, "it could be a really long day for us."

Alabama Coach Nick Saban talks to Alabama defensive back Justin Woodall (27) during the second quarter against LSU.

nick

Looking Back at Saban's West Virginia Roots

By Paul Gattis

The sun had fallen behind the trees on a July evening, the lingering glow from a sweltering summer day slowing the arriving darkness.

The visit to the Mount Carmel Cemetery was ending and Tom Hulderman was starting back to the car. Then he stopped.

"To this day," Hulderman said earlier, "I put flowers on his grave every year."

As he prepared to leave the cemetery, Hulderman looked down and - with emotions thundering through his mind - lightly patted Nick Saban's tombstone.

Then with a certain determination, the lifelong friend of Nick Saban Jr. walked away before stopping again.

"Do you mind if I smoke?" Hulderman asked a visitor.

The nerves. They needed calming.

To go back to Nick Saban Jr.'s past, to learn more about the new Alabama football coach, the journey leads you here to this picturesque hillside graveyard just outside of the town Saban calls his own.

Permeating every conversation about Nick Saban Jr. - known as "Brother" here in this coal-mining region about 90 miles south of Pittsburgh - is Nick Saban Sr.

The field where Alabama's coach first learned about football is now called Nick Saban Memorial Field.

When Saban Sr. died suddenly of a heart attack in 1973 and his new widow insisted that the Idamay Black Diamonds

- the Pop Warner team he founded - play the next day as scheduled, the league instead said, "Forget it. Nobody's playing. All games are canceled."

"Besides my father," Hulderman said, "Nick Sr. is the greatest person I ever met in my life."

"I've never had a mentor like Nick Saban Sr.," said Joe Manchin, a childhood friend of the younger Saban's who is now the governor of West Virginia.

Then Manchin said the words that could chill the Crimson Tide nation right down to its houndstooth heart:

"What little bit I know about Bear Bryant, (Saban) came probably as close as any human being to being raised under the same mental toughness as a Bear Bryant with his father.

"If you want someone who is conditioned and understands the toughness it's going to take to succeed at that level without Bear Bryant being his father, he had someone as tough, if not tougher, to make sure he was molded into the right person. So he's got all the ingredients to do the job."

A mile from Monongah

It's a bit misleading to say that Fairmont is Saban's hometown. He actually grew up about nine miles south of town on U.S. Route 19 and about a mile from the community of Monongah, where he went to high school.

The service station his dad ran is still there more than 30 years after his death, though it no longer pumps gas and is now a rundown repair shop.

The ice cream shop/restaurant operated by his mother, Mary, is still there, too, just across the street. The Saban home is still there, a small, one-story brick dwelling just to the side and behind the service station.

This slice of Saban's childhood world might well be described as down in a hollow, where state road 218 charts a northwest track from Route 19 toward the tiny communities of Idamay and Farmington, which is Manchin's hometown.

It's out in the country, out in the sticks, a place so swallowed up by mountains and remoteness that a cell phone is nothing more than a paperweight.

This is where Nick Saban became who he is today.

Willie Criado would know. The postmaster in Idamay for 38 years and now retired, he and Saban's father shared June 11, 1927, as their birthday as well as lockers in school in Farmington.

When Saban Sr. founded the Black Diamonds, Criado was his right-hand man. And when his friend died, Criado was the one who told his wife.

"Nick was the type of guy who, if he had something on his mind, might walk right by you and say nothing," Criado said. "Then on the way back, he'd get to talking to you like it never happened. That's just the way he was."

Kerry Marbury would know. He and Saban are also lifelong friends and, even though Marbury is African-American, they were each other's best man at their weddings.

"I felt sorry for 'Brother' because he got treated worse than anybody," Marbury said, laughing at the memory. "Everybody else got the love and he got scrutinized.

"They used to watch film (of football games) when film was not even a part of life. They had this 8 mm film and they would say 'Want to stay and watch?' And I would say, 'Noooo, thanks.'"

Playing for ice cream

Nick Saban's dad, in fact, seemed like a community father.

He somehow came up with the money to buy a used bus, which he drove to the various small pockets of people outside Fairmont to pick up their children for football practice. Monongah, Idamay, Farmington, Carolina, Number Nine.

Then after practice - he would take them all back home again.

"I always admired the fact that he would come to every little coal mining community," said Marbury, now a teacher at Fairmont State University who lived in Carolina.

It all started in 1962 when Saban's father wanted to join the Pop Warner League in Fairmont, which had four teams. One of the teams was disbanded and the black and orange uniforms were sent to Idamay - a sort of hub for the rural area south of town.

It's possible the uniforms were simply given to the Black Diamonds. But Criado isn't certain that Saban Sr. didn't just buy them himself and not tell anyone.

Alabama Coach Nick Saban celebrates after the 26-21 defeat of Auburn at Jordan-Hare Stadium.

STAFF PHOTO/MARK ALMOND

The plan was for a couple of college kids to coach the Black Diamonds while Saban just kept a parental eye on the team as the commissioner and Criado the secretary.

But the college kids didn't show up and so Saban became the coach himself. The Black Diamonds didn't win a game that first year but went 5-5 the next and were undefeated and unscored upon the next.

Along the way, there was a 39-game winning streak and two shutout wins over a team from Pennsylvania that had a kid named Joe Montana as its quarterback.

"Nick was a helluva coach," Criado said.

"He had a Dairy Queen and he said if you guys win, we'll go to Dairy Queen after the game," said Marbury, who enjoyed a long career in the Canadian Football League after starring at the University of West Virginia.

"We almost broke him after a few years. I tell people today that I enjoyed playing for that ice cream more than I did money. I really did. I looked forward to going to the Dairy Queen."

And he could motivate with fear.

"We were in this one particular game and things weren't going too good," Criado said. "He had this clipboard with the plays on it. He walked in the dressing room and threw that thing against the wall and the papers went everywhere and those kids were scared to death. Out the door he went and he didn't say a word. I'd never seen him do that before.

"I just sat there for a while and waited to see if he was going to come back. It looked like he wasn't going to do it so I got to talking to them and I said 'Let's go

out there and show him we can win this ballgame.' And they like to broke down the door."

But coaching may have killed him, too.

Criado said he knew his friend had a heart problem, knew that doctors encouraged him to give up coaching. Still, he refused to surrender.

On Sept. 22, 1973, while their son was attending Kent State, Nick and Mary Saban were driving back home. As they got within a mile or so of the house, Nick asked to get out so he could jog the rest of the way.

Soon Criado and Mary Saban were following an ambulance to the hospital and waiting together in the emergency room.

"Somebody (at the hospital) paged her, somebody was on the phone," Criado said. "It was Brother. She went to the phone. About that time, the nurse came and told me he was gone and wanted to know if I wanted to see him.

"I said, 'No, I don't want to see him like that.' "

'No man stands as tall'

It's almost as if you can see each domino falling that led Nick Saban to Alabama, as if his first 55 years were merely a preparation for the task he now faces, though that's far too presumptuous and far too simplistic.

It's easy to imagine friends actually competing to see who can make Saban laugh first. Usually, it's Manchin and Joe Pendry, the Tide's offensive line coach and Manchin's roommate from his days at West Virginia.

"It's hard to get him to laugh because he's so serious," Manchin said. "We kid about it. Joe and I always kid about who can make Brother laugh quicker and we never know who wins because it takes a while.

"I can get him to break down pretty quick because I know enough to get him to go."

But behind every coerced laugh, behind every cha-ching of his college football record $32 million contract, there are the roots of West Virginia.

"His father was truly the toughest, yet the most compassionate person and most caring and loving person," Manchin said. "But you really had to look for all of that because he was tough."

That's why Hulderman wiped tears from his eyes remembering his childhood with the Sabans before making the emotional trip to the cemetery.

"I get emotional when I talk about him," Hulderman said of Saban. "He's a great person. His parents were like my second parents. When his father died, it was a hard day."

Indeed, the tombstone carries this epithet: "No man stands as tall as when he stoops to help a child."

Maybe that final domino has fallen and Saban - with 55 years of preparation - has arrived at this moment in life destined to deliver a championship for a fan base that's seemingly been aching for a winner since Bryant died more than 24 years ago.

"He is not trying to be the next Bear Bryant," Manchin said. "He's going to be the first Nick Saban."

assistant coaches

scott cochran

Head Football Strength and Conditioning Coach
Cochran joined the Alabama staff in 2007 after spending three seasons with the NBA New Orleans Hornets as assistant strength coach. Before that, Cochran worked for his alma mater, Louisiana State, as assistant strength coach for the 2003 National Champion Tiger football team. A native of New Orleans, Cochran received a bachelor's degree in kinesiology from LSU in 2001 and added a master's degree in sports management from LSU in 2003.

sal sunseri
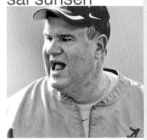

Assistant Head Coach/Linebackers
Sunseri joined Alabama in January 2009 after coaching NFL Carolina Panthers' defensive line. Prior to Carolina, Sunseri was linebackers coach and special teams coordinator at Michigan State in 2001 and Louisiana State in 2000. He also has coached at Louisville, Alabama A&M, Illinois State and Iowa Wesleyan. He was a 1978 walk-on at Pittsburgh and ended his career as team captain and consensus All-American linebacker in 1981. He received a communications degree from Pittsburgh in 1982.

james willis

Associate Head Coach/Linebackers
A seven-year NFL veteran, Willis joined Alabama in January 2009 after coaching linebackers at Auburn for three years. Prior to Auburn, Willis coached linebackers at Temple (2005) and Rhode Island (2004-05). The three-year Auburn starter was a Parade All-American and All-SEC selection in 1992. He played professionally for Green Bay (2003-04), Philadelphia (1995-98) where he was a three-year starter for the Eagles, and, his final NFL season in 1999, with Seattle.

bobby williams

Tight Ends/Special Teams
A veteran coach with both college and NFL experience, Williams joined Nick Saban's coaching staff as tight ends coach and special teams coordinator in January 2008. The 1982 Purdue graduate previously worked with Saban at Michigan State, LSU and the Miami Dolphins. He was a four-year letterman for the Boilermakers, starting his career as a running back before moving to defensive back and being named a tri-captain his senior year.

kirby smart

Defensive Coordinator/Secondary
Kirby Smart joined the Crimson Tide football staff in January, 2007, after coaching safeties for the Miami Dolphins in 2006. Before that, Smart spent six years coaching at Georgia (1999 and 2005), LSU (2004), Florida State (2002-03), and Valdosta State (2000-01). At Georgia, Smart lettered four-year at defensive back, and was first-team All-SEC as a senior. Smart earned his undergraduate degree in finance from Georgia and master's degree from Florida State.

Assistant Head Coach/Offensive Line
The 19-year NFL coaching veteran joined Alabama in January, 2007 after coaching the Houston Texans offensive line and coordinating the offense. Prior to that, he worked three years for the Carolina Panthers. The West Virginia native played two seasons at West Virginia (1965-66) before a career-ending injury. His college coaching career includes West Virginia, Kansas State, Pittsburgh and Michigan State. He also coached in the USFL with the Philadelphia Stars and Pittsburgh Maulers.

Offensive Coordinator/Quarterbacks
McElwain came to Alabama in January 2009 from the same position at Fresno State. He spent the 2006 season in the NFL as quarterbacks coach for the Oakland Raiders. He also coached receivers and special teams at Michigan State and Louisville and, before that, was offensive coordinator, quarterbacks and receivers coach at Montana State, and quarterbacks and receivers coach at Eastern Washington where, as a 1980s student, played quarterback and earned an Education degree.

Defensive Line
Bo Davis joined the Crimson Tide in January, 2007, after serving as an assistant strength and conditioning coach in 2006 and assistant defensive line coach with the Miami Dolphins under Nick Saban. Prior to the Dolphins, the Magee, Miss. was an assistant strength and conditioning coach for Saban and current LSU coach Les Miles from 2002-05 at LSU where he played from 1990 to 1992, earning all-SEC honors as a nose guard.

Receivers/Recruiting Coordinator
The former North Carolina State tight ends coach, recruiting coordinator and quarterbacks coach joined the Alabama staff in February 2007 as receivers coach and recruiting coordinator. With more than a quarter century of college coaching experience, Cignetti served as recruiting coordinator at Pittsburgh from 1994-99, and also coached quarterbacks. Other coaching stints for the West Virginia graduate include Temple, Rice and Davidson. He played quarterback at West Virginia from 1979-82.

Associate Head Coach/Running Backs
Burton Burns joined the Alabama coaching staff in January 2007 after eight seasons as an assistant coach at Clemson. Prior to that, the New Orleans native spent five years at Tulane, including the 1998 12-0 season. Burns played fullback from 1971-75 at Nebraska under Coach Tom Osborne and participated in the Orange Bowl, Cotton Bowl and Sugar Bowl. He earned a bachelor's degree in education from Nebraska in 1976.

joe pendry

jim mcelwain

bo davis

curt cignetti

burton burns

pre
season

Terrence Cody (62), right, runs through drills with Josh Chapman (99) during the University of Alabama football practice in Tuscaloosa on Thursday, Aug. 6, 2009.

STAFF PHOTO/MICHELLE WILLIAMS

Two-loss Ending to 2008 Has Crimson Tide Working for Stronger Finish

By GENTRY ESTES

Despite an SEC West title, unbeaten regular season and first victory over Auburn in seven tries, Alabama linebacker Rolando McClain recalls the 2008 season in one word: "Disappointed."

"But this year will be different," McClain said.

After year one, Crimson Tide coach Nick Saban hung up the final scores of losses to Mississippi State and Louisiana-Monroe all over the locker room.

Now when he should be hard up for reliable offseason motivation, Saban actually didn't have to look very far. For all the success of the previous season, Alabama still carries a two-game losing streak into the Sept. 5 opener against Virginia Tech in Atlanta.

Alabama's 12-game run last season was spoiled by eventual national champ Florida in the SEC title game. Worse was an embarrassing Sugar Bowl no-show against Utah. Saban has made sure it hasn't been overlooked.

"Coach Saban is preaching to us, 'Finish, finish, finish,'" McClain said.

"When we're running our 110s, guys are screaming, 'See what happened at the end of the season?'" cornerback/return man Javier Arenas said.

"And we're motivated and run faster."

Crimson Tide players profess they still seek to prove a point in year three of Saban's tenure, though the second edition was certainly a leap back toward national prominence, with victories fueled by a team that was blessed with few injuries and experience in the right places.

Quarterback John Parker Wilson was solid and battle-tested enough to win the tough games. Left offensive tackle Andre Smith was voted the best lineman in the nation. Center Antoine Caldwell was an All-American. So was safety Rashad Johnson, who directed much of the defense. Tailback Glen Coffee stayed healthy and was a handful to deal with all season.

All those players are now gone, with Smith and Coffee leaving a year early and the others also trying their fortunes in the NFL.

"We had fantastic leadership last year. We had some guys that were as good a leader as you're ever going to find," Saban said.

"I don't think leadership just comes from seniors. You have players who are very good players that can be of any age that can affect other people. I think it's important that players don't think they have to be seniors to affect other people."

Defensively, Alabama should be just fine. It returns eight starters from a group that was second against the run and seventh nationally in scoring defense. Even without Johnson, the cupboard is stacked with the likes of Arenas, McClain, linebacker Dont'a Hightower and nose tackle Terrence Cody.

"We've got a lot of talented players back, and they can't become complacent," defensive coordinator Kirby Smart said. "We've got to continue to work hard and those guys are doing a good job of teaching the younger guys."

Offensively, the line replaces three starters and is the biggest area of concern on the squad. Untested junior quarterback Greg McElroy steps in for Wilson, and there are proven veterans at running back.

But Alabama is now primarily banking on Saban's past two signing classes — both of which were rated among the nation's elite — to fill out the rest of the lineup. Can the youngsters mature in time to fulfill promise for another national title run?

Some already have. Tailback Mark Ingram and Hightower sprang from the gate toward starring roles last season.

But no one was near wide receiver Julio Jones, a former Foley standout who put himself among the country's best while secretly battling injuries all season.

"It would be nice to have a lot of young players who watch some of that and see that effort and that toughness," Saban said.

Now after three offseason surgeries, Jones said he's finally healthy. Alabama, in turn, is moving Jones around more and working on additional ways to supply him the football.

"It's coming real easy to me now," Jones said. "For me being here a year, I already knew half the positions. So I could learn more routes and different things at the other positions."

Alabama was ranked fifth in the season's first USA Today coaches poll. Virginia Tech, though, was seventh.

While the Hokies are a large hurdle in the season's opening game, Saban claims he wouldn't prefer it any other way.

"It'll be a challenging game for every facet of our team," Saban said. "I think it helps your offseason. The players are more intense about what they're doing because they know they're preparing for a huge challenge in the first game."

Shades of '92?

Crimson Tide defense wants to rank with school's best

By DON KAUSLER JR.

The 1978-79 defenses were good. The 1961 defense was better. But in the modern Alabama football era, conversations about great defense often begin and end with the 1992 Crimson Tide.

The 2008 defense was good. The 2009 defense could be better. It wants to be great. It wants to rank with the best in school history.

Can it outdo '92?

John Copeland...Eric Curry...George Teague...Antonio Langham.

The '78 defense, immortalized by the "Goal-Line Stand" in a Sugar Bowl showdown against topranked Penn State, had its own impressive roll call of NFL first-round draft choice.

Barry Krauss...Marty Lyons...Don Mc-Neal...E.J. Junior.

The '61 defense is legendary because it allowed only 25 points in 11 games, including six shutouts (five consecutive games). It didn't produce first-round draft picks, but two stars are in the college football Hall of Fame, Lee Roy Jordan and Billy Neighbors.

Now here comes the 2009 defense, violently ready to make its mark. It is big, fast and strong. And it is starstudded.

Rolando McClain...Terrence Cody...Dont'a Hightower...Javier Arenas.

The season starts at 7 p.m. Sept. 5 when fifthranked Alabama collides with seventh-ranked Virginia Tech in Atlanta.

Let the coronation begin?...No so fast.

"Where it is now, we gave up 31 points in (each of) the last two games we played," said Alabama coach Nick Saban, reflecting on a 31-20 loss to Florida in the Southeastern Conference championship game and a 31-17 loss to Utah in the Sugar Bowl."

"Even though we were going against two of the best offenses in the country, we need to do better. There's a lot of room for improvement," Saban added.

His players understand.

Changes in the defensive coaching staff appear to be making a difference. Lance Thompson has moved on to Tennessee. Kevin Steele has moved on to Clemson. Sal Sunseri left the Carolina Panthers to coach the Tide's outside linebackers. In a coup for Saban, James Willis left Auburn to coach the Tide's inside linebackers.

"I love Coach Sal and Coach Willis," Hightower said. "They've turned it up a few notches."

Eight starters return from a defense that led the Tide to a 12-0 regular season. They don't include Washington, a 6-foot-5, 290-pound senior who started at nose guard in 2007. He replaces defensive end Bobby Greenwood.

"I really don't consider myself a new guy," Washington said. "I was a starter two years ago. I think of myself as a costarter last year."

Moving from the inside of the line to the outside isn't a problem.

Experience at nose guard "helps me be able to play the run tougher," Washington said.

"When I was rushing the quarterback from the nose, I was blocked by two or three people. Now I'm against a single blocker. I feel if I'm blocked by a single guy, I'm going to win."

Linebackers are the Tide's strength. The monsters are McClain and Hightower.

"It's hard enough for another team to game plan for a Rolando McClain," Washington said, "but now they've got to game plan for Rolando McClain and Dont'a Hightower."

Sophomore running back Mark Ingram sympathizes with opponents. He runs against this defense in practice and scrimmages. He smiled when asked which players hit the hardest.

"Those two in the middle," he said, "25 (McClain) and 30 (Hightower)."

Common denominators such as statistics, points allowed and draft choices aside, the ultimate measurement of the 1961, '78, '79 and '92 defenses was winning. Each unit led Alabama to a national championship.

That's a tough act for the 2009 defense to follow.

"I don't want to look toward the end of the season," Washington said, "but if we're looked back on as one of the best defenses ever here, that's something I'll hold dear to my heart."

Alabama quarterback Greg McElroy (12) looks to pass during practice in the indoor facility in Tuscaloosa, Ala., Thursday Aug. 20, 2009.

STAFF PHOTO/MARK ALMOND

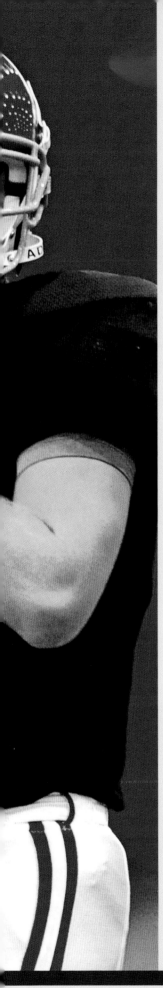

McElroy Gets His Shot as Alabama's Quarterback

By GENTRY ESTES

It has been a long offseason, filled with film study, anticipation and an increasingly neglected girlfriend who has started teasing Greg McElroy that he has changed.

Hey, he doesn't hate the fame that comes with being the starting quarterback at the University of Alabama, but he said he's determined not to let it turn him into something he's not.

"You won't see me changing as far as the way I handle myself and control myself," McElroy said. "I refuse to let that happen.

"My time was dedicated to the team and improving myself. I spent a lot of time watching film both of our own offense and some of the opponents we'll be facing in the upcoming weeks."

Finally, he's the guy. And while coach Nick Saban never came right out and said McElroy won the competition during spring camp to become Alabama's new No. 1 quarterback, he never had to.

There was never much doubt who would take the wheel from three-year starter John Parker Wilson and lead a program in the final steps of a return from mediocrity back to the national spotlight.

He made it clear on the field, leading his side to an A-Day victory at Bryant-Denny Stadium.

He's also made it clear off of it, shedding the choir boy persona to rally the troops with salty lingo at halftime of that spring game.

"He's really a vocal guy," left guard Mike Johnson said. "We've really been impressed with him, and I think that's why a lot of people in the media hear that he's going to be impressive, because he's taken such good control."

McElroy has since made a trip to the Manning family's passing academy, where he received tips from Archie, Peyton and Eli while rooming with Texas quarterback Colt McCoy and Oklahoma's Sam Bradford, a pair of Heisman Trophy frontrunners.

"It was a great opportunity for me," McElroy said, "and I know I came back a better player than when I went there."

Along the way, there has never been any notion that this was not McElroy's team in 2009.

"He has really deserved, I think, the shot in what he's doing right now," offensive coordinator Jim McElwain said.

Patiently and without objection, McElroy waited

almost three years. He prepared game after game for an eventuality that never came.

Wilson didn't miss a start in three years because of injury, a remarkable streak of durability that left McElroy content to signal in plays from the sideline, hoping for a lead large enough to allow him a few handoffs or throws before time expired.

It's not that his time has been wasted, though. Before ever taking a snap as the Crimson Tide's starting quarterback, McElroy earned his undergraduate degree and enrolled in graduate school.

"He is very smart," Saban said. "Players really like him. He has a lot of positive leadership qualities, and he does affect other people."

With the Crimson Tide barreling toward the Sept. 5 season opener against highly regarded Virginia Tech, who really knows what to expect when Alabama's new quarterback finally gets that first collegiate start?

"It's understandable," McElroy said. "A lot of people don't know what to expect, and I don't expect them to expect anything. I don't expect coaches to expect anything.

"They're going to put me in a position to make a play, and I'm looking forward to that. As far as my expectations for myself, I can't say I have any either.

"Just go out there and enjoy the situation and take every moment like it's your last and just have fun with it."

McElroy takes comfort in the fact that he was in a similar situation in high school. He sat behind future Missouri star Chase Daniel until his senior year, when he led Southlake Carroll (Texas) High School to a state championship. He completed 21-of-31 passes for 328 yards in the title game, finishing the year with a staggering 4,687 passing yards and 56 touchdowns.

But the lack of playing time at Alabama has offered precious few hints about McElroy's ability. He has participated in only eight games, all in mop-up duty. He had thrown only 20 passes — completing 16 — for two touchdowns and 196 yards.

"He's not as experienced as J.P. was, but he's taking on the opportunity head-strong," receiver Mike McCoy said.

"All we can do is just look for him, and he's going to surprise a lot of people out there."

Surprise?

"He can't help but surprise us, because nobody knows what to expect," McCoy said.

"We just feel like he's the man. He's our Superman."

va. tech

Alabama running back Mark Ingram (22) dives over Virginia Tech defenders for extra yardage in the fourth quarter of the Chick-fil-A Kickoff Game.

CRIMSON TIDE | 34
HOKIES | 24

09.05.09 | 7 p.m. | Georgia Dome | Atlanta, GA

Home in the Dome

Ingram, Alabama wear down Virginia Tech

By GENTRY ESTES

In methods and makeup, this appears to be a much different Alabama football team from the one that visited the Georgia Dome to open last season.

The ultimate goal, however, stayed the same.

"Just hit them in the mouth until they can't take it anymore," Crimson Tide linebacker Dont'a Hightower said.

Fifth-ranked Alabama dug deep Saturday night to overcome a deficit in the final quarter and secure a 34-24 victory over seventh-ranked Virginia Tech in the marquee matchup of college football's opening weekend.

The contest wasn't the defensive struggle many projected. It actually turned into a shootout with two stout yet tiring defenses in the fourth quarter, and Alabama clearly managed more firepower early and late.

The Crimson Tide dominated the statistics sheet, but needed a series of late game-turning plays to finally overcome its own mishaps and put away the defending Atlantic Coast Conference champion Hokies.

"We knew we would have to earn it against these guys," Alabama coach Nick Saban said, "and we had to earn it. It was a tough game and it was probably a good thing our team had to go through that. ... This team responded to a lot of adversity in the game and overcame themselves."

"I've never been so happy after a start," quarterback Greg McElroy said.

What kind of Crimson Tide showed Saturday night?

Through the lens of last season, it was remarkably different. Alabama's defense is still solid. It's still punishing against the run, though susceptible to the big plays when it wasn't for most of last year.

Workhorse tailback Mark Ingram was named the game's most valuable offensive player, carrying 26 times for 150 yards, while Roy Upchurch added 90 yards on 7 attempts. The Crimson Tide actually outgained the Hokies 498 yards to 155, including a whopping 268-64 difference on the ground.

"That's kind of crazy," nose tackle Terrence Cody said when told the difference.

ap top 10 released 09.06.09

Alabama linebacker Courtney Upshaw (41) (left) and Alabama defensive back Robby Green (23) hit Virginia Tech's Davon Morgan (2) forcing him to fumble on a fourth-quarter kickoff return.

STAFF PHOTO/MARK ALMOND

TEAM	1ST	2ND	3RD	4TH	FINAL
ALABAMA	9	7	0	18	34
VIRGINIA TECH	7	10	0	7	24

Attendance   74,954 Georgia Dome

SCORING SUMMARY

UA   L Tiffin 49 yd field goal, 6 plays, 26 yds, TOP 3:10
UA   L Tiffin 34 yd field goal, 7 plays, 30 yds, TOP 1:59
VT   D Roberts 98 yd kickoff return (M Waldron kick)
UA   L Tiffin 32 yd field goal, 4 plays, 2 yds, TOP 0:39
VT   M Waldron, 28 yd field goal, 4 plays, 3 yds, TOP 2:00
UA   R Upchurch 19 yd run (L Tiffin kick), 11 plays, 76 yds, TOP 5:24
VT   R Williams 1 yd run (M Waldron kick), 7 plays, 51 yds, TOP 2:01
UA   M Ingram 6 yd run (C Peek pass from G McElroy), 2 plays, 54 yds, TOP 0:37
UA   L Tiffin 20 yd field goal, 5 plays, 17 yards, TOP 1:45
VT   R Williams 32 yd run (M Waldron kick). 2 plays, 37 yds, TOP 1:00
UA   M Ingram 18 yd pass from G McElroy (L Tiffin kick), 5 plays, 74 yds, TOP 2:40

TEAM STATISTICS

	UA	VT
FIRST DOWNS	22	11
NET YARDS RUSHING	268	64
NET YARDS PASSING	230	91
COMPLETIONS-ATTEMPTS-INT	15-30-1	9-20-0
TOTAL OFFENSE YARDS	498	155
PENALTIES: NUMBER-YARDS	10-83	6-45
PUNTS-YARDS	5-44.8	8-45.6
PUNT RETURNS: NUMBER-YDS-TD	3-35-0	2-11-0
KICKOFF RETURNS: NUMBER-YDS-TD	5-99-0	8-243-1
POSSESSION TIME	36:32	22:19
SACKS BY: NUMBER-YARDS LOST	5-38	2-5
FIELD GOALS	4-5	1-1
FUMBLES: NUMBER-LOST	2-1	5-2

INDIVIDUAL OFFENSIVE STATISTICS

RUSHING: UA — M Ingram 26-150; R Upchurch 7-90; G McElroy 8-28;
                      T Richardson 3-10; T Grant 2-2;
                      VT — R Williams 13-71; J Oglesby 6-16; D Coale 1-5; T Taylor 10 (-26)
PASSING: UA — G McElroy 30-15-1, 230   VT — T Taylor 20-9-0, 91
RECEIVING: UA — J Jones 4-46; D Hanks 3-55; C Peek 3-37; M Ingram 3-35;
                      M Maze 2-57
                      VT — J Boykin 3-19; R Williams 2-42; D Coale 2-16; J Oglesby 2-14

INDIVIDUAL DEFENSIVE STATISTICS

INTERCEPTIONS: VT — A Hopkins 1
SACKS   UA — R McClain 2; M Dareus 1; J Arenas 1;
                  VT — J Worlds 1
TACKLES: UA — R McClain 4-1; E Anders 3-5; J Arenas 3-2; M Johnson 3-0;
                  D Hightower 2-4
                  VT — J Johnson 9-4; S Virgil 7-2; C Grimm 5-3; B Rivers 4-7; K Chancellor 3-1

1	2	3	4	5	6	7	8	9	10
FLORIDA	TEXAS	USC	ALABAMA	OKLAHOMA STATE	MISSISSIPPI	PENN STATE	OHIO STATE	BRIGHAM YOUNG	CALIFORNIA

Alabama linebacker Rolando McClain (25) sacks Virginia Tech quarterback Tyrod Taylor (5) in the fourth quarter of the game.

STAFF PHOTO/
MARK ALMOND

As Cody suggested, it just didn't seem so easy.

Gone were the days when Alabama seemingly never trailed. Gone was a plodding offense that could simply maul an opposing defense with its line and running backs, thus controlling and killing a game between the tackles.

This Crimson Tide offense got creative. It relied more on big plays, quick strikes and trickery behind an offensive line that is now without All-Americans Andre Smith and Antoine Caldwell.

Yes, Alabama now is an offense that puts Ingram in the shotgun for a direct snap on the game's first play and throws on third-and-1.

It's also an offense that when it gets rolling, it's capable of quickly putting away a tight game against a top-10 opponent.

Things weren't really going our way for a while," McElroy said. "We needed to step up and make a play."

Alabama trailed 17-16 when McElroy trotted back onto the field near the 12:50 mark of the fourth quarter. He was bruised from a night's worth of pressure and punishment cooked up by Virginia Tech defensive coordinator Bud Foster, having missed nine consecutive throws at one point in the first half.

But McElroy didn't miss his next one, delivering a 46-yard strike in stride to receiver Marquis Maze.

"I think he played better as the game went on," Saban said of McElroy. "I think his confidence got better."

On the next snap, Ingram burst 6 yards into the end zone to regain a lead that was extended to seven when McElroy found Colin Peek on the 2-point conversion.

On the ensuing kickoff, Alabama's Chris Rogers stripped Virginia Tech return man Davon Morgan. The fumble set up a Leigh Tiffin field goal, extending the lead to 27-17.

Ever the special teams power, Virginia Tech countered with a long kickoff return that ultimately led to a touchdown. But Alabama needed only five plays to answer again.

With 9:08 to play, Ingram dashed 39 yards down the left sideline. He then rumbled 18 yards on a short pass from McElroy for the touchdown that began sending a vocal contingent of Virginia Tech fans toward the exits.

"You've got to kind of take a step back and talk to yourself," McElroy said. "I was doing that throughout. ... As the game progressed, they got a little tired. I think that's where our offseason condition and hard work paid off.

"We were still going strong."

Deaderick's return from shooting inspires teammates

By Mike Herndon

Five days ago, Brandon Deaderick was laid up in a Tuscaloosa hospital with a bullet in his arm, thankful to be alive.

On Saturday night, he stood in uniform on the sidelines as his Alabama teammates took the field at the Georgia Dome for the Chick-fil-A Kickoff Game. That he was here, cleared by a doctor to make the trip and dress out, was amazing.

Then, late in the first quarter, Deaderick left the sidelines and went into the game. He played only a handful of series, a white sleeve on his arm, but to his Alabama teammates who earlier in the week worried whether he'd ever be able to rejoin them at all, just his presence on the field meant the world.

"It inspired us a lot," said Alabama nose tackle Terrence Cody. "We're all brothers, the whole defensive line — we do everything together. To have him out there just hyped us up and got us ready."

Five days ago, Deaderick was sitting with a female friend in a car outside a Northport apartment complex when a man in dark clothes approached the car. Deaderick got out to confront the threat, to protect his friend. A scuffle ensued, Deaderick was shot in the forearm and the shooter fled.

Had the trajectory of that bullet been altered a few inches, had the angle of the shot been tipped even slightly, Deaderick might not be here at all today. Alabama players might have had to enter Saturday's game mourning the loss of a friend and teammate instead of simply wondering if or how much he would play.

"I was trying to find a way not to play him, but he wanted to play so we spot-played him," coach Nick Saban said. "I think the players really wanted him to play. I think the fact that he was with us at practice Thursday and was able to be out there tonight was a good thing."

For most of the game Saturday, the Crimson Tide defense played like it was inspired. It held Virginia Tech to only 68 yards in the first half and 155 overall. It sacked

Hokies quarterback Tyrod Taylor five times and harassed him on several others. It kept Alabama in the game when its offense sputtered or its special teams broke down.

With the exception of a few dumb penalties — including two on one play by Rolando McClain — and two big breakdowns, one in the secondary in the first half and one against the run in the second, it largely kept Virginia Tech in check.

Deaderick didn't show up much on the stat sheet Saturday night, but he will be able to contribute more in the coming weeks. The important thing was that he showed up at all.

He's a leader," Cody said, "and he showed it just by playing."

fla   tnl.

CRIMSON TIDE | 40

GOLDEN PANTHERS | 14

09.12.09 | 6 p.m. | Bryant-Denny Stadium | Tuscaloosa, AL

Alabama running back Trent Richardson (3) runs over Florida International cornerback Jeremiah Weatherspoon (6) in the first quarter.

STAFF PHOTO/ MARK ALMOND

Something Old, Something New, Something Good for Crimson Tide

By DOUG SEGREST

With two top offensive weapons down and FIU bidding for an upset, Alabama resorted to an old wives tale.

Or at least an old bridal superstition: something old, something new.

Something old, as in senior receiver Mike McCoy. Something new, as in true freshman running back Trent Richardson.

Something good: a 40-14 Alabama victory after a too-close-for-comfort first half.

With Julio Jones out before halftime with a bruised knee, McCoy turned in his biggest night since arriving on campus, reaching the 100-yard plateau for the first time. Statistically, he did all his damage in the first half, combining with quarterback Greg McElroy for five catches and 100 yards receiving to keep the Tide offense moving.

Even though McCoy was one of Alabama's go-to options a year ago, he never caught more than five passes or had more than 47 yards receiving before Saturday's breakout performance.

"Mike McCoy had a 100-yard plus game after Julio went down," Tide coach Nick Saban said. "Most of the passes we threw to him were intended for No. 8."

Credit McElroy, as well. At one point, he set a school record, completing 14 straight passes. But it was clear that, with Jones out, the Double Mac Attack could be effective.

As for the ground assault, first-team running back Mark Ingram played some after opening the game on the bench. Ingram took a hit on his knee on his final carry of the Virginia Tech game. Back to practice Monday, he missed the next two practices with the flu.

Enter Richardson, who ran for two touchdowns and finished with a career-best 118 yards on 15 carries.

"Trent did a great job," Ingram said. "I'm not surprised at all. He's been doing it all fall. Hes a great running back."

With Alabama holding a harrowing 20-14 lead at the half, Richardson helped bust the game open after the teams returned to the field. He made it 26-14 late in the third with a 9-yard run.

After Javier Arenas returned a punt 46 yards following the next FIU possession, Richardson put the game out of reach with a 35-yard jaunt into the end zone.

"It's all about the talent level and all the hard work those guys have put in," left guard Mike Johnson said. "We try to get guys to work hard every day, because you never know when youll be called on."

While McCoy and Richardson shined in a new spotlight, McElroy threw for 203 yards in the first half alone. And an offensive line that includes three new starters in 2009 allowed just one quarterback sack.

"The sky's the limit with this offense," McElroy said. "We don't think were scratching the surface."

ap top 10 released 09.13.09

Alabama defensive lineman Terrence Cody (62), linebacker Rolando McClain (25) and defensive lineman Lorenzo Washington (97) wrap up Florida International running back Darriet Perry (28) in the first quarter.

STAFF PHOTO/MARK ALMOND

TEAM	1ST	2ND	3RD	4TH	FINAL
ALABAMA	10	10	6	14	40
FLA. INTERNATIONAL	7	7	0	0	14

Attendance   92,012 Bryant-Denny Stadium

SCORING SUMMARY

UA   L Tiffin 23 yd field goal, 13 plays, 55 yards, TOP 5:58
UA   M McCoy 24 yd pass from G McElroy (L Tiffin kick), 7 plays, 80 yds, TOP 3:20
FIU T Hilton 96 yd kickoff return (D Rivest kick)
UA   L Tiffin 29 yd field goal, 7 plays, 50 yds, TOP 3:12
FIU G Ellingson 9 yd pass from P McCall (D Rivest kick), 8 plays, 60 yds, TOP 4:26
UA   M Ingram 2 yd run (L Tiffin kick), 5 plays, 69 yds, TOP 2:09
UA   T Richardson 9 yd run, (G McElroy pass failed), 7 plays, 50 yds, TOP 2:11
UA   T Richardson 35 yd run (L Tiffin kick), 2 plays, 40 yards, TOP 0:18
UA   T Grant 42 yd run (L Tiffin kick), 3 plays, 54 yds, TOP 1:35

TEAM STATISTICS

	UA	FIU
FIRST DOWNS	26	13
NET YARDS RUSHING	275	1
NET YARDS PASSING	241	213
COMPLETIONS-ATTEMPTS-INT	18-24-0	18-38-1
TOTAL OFFENSE YARDS	516	214
PENALTIES: NUMBER-YARDS	7-65	8-54
PUNTS-YARDS	3-129	8-379
PUNT RETURNS: NUMBER-YDS-TD	4-101-0	1-3-0
KICKOFF RETURNS: NUMBER-YDS-TD	2-30-0	7-185-1
POSSESSION TIME	31:38	28:04
SACKS BY: NUMBER-YARDS LOST	5-38	1-15
FIELD GOALS	2-3	0-0
FUMBLES: NUMBER-LOST	1-0	2-0

INDIVIDUAL OFFENSIVE STATISTICS

RUSHING: UA – T Richardson 15-118; T Grant 6-69; M Ingram 10-56;
           D Goode 4-24; R Upchurch 4-17; J Jones 1-5
           FIU – D Mallary 3-13; W Younger, 2-12; D Perry 9-5; T Hilton 1-0; G
           McCall 11-(-29)
PASSING: UA – G McElroy 24-18-0, 241
           FIU – P McCall 32-16-0, 189; W Younger 6-2-1, 24
RECEIVING: UA – M McCoy 5-100; M Ingram 4-47; T Richardson 2-23;
           E Alexander 2-20; P Dial 1-19; C Peek 1-13; D Hanks 1-11; J Jones 1-9;
           B Smelley 1-(-1)
           FIU – G Ellingson 5-92; T Hilton 5-40; D Perry 3-14; J Frierson 2-22;
           C Anderson 1-23; M Rolle 1-16; J Faucher 1-6

INDIVIDUAL DEFENSIVE STATISTICS

INTERCEPTIONS: UA –M Barron 1-17
SACKS: UA – M Dareus 2-0; M Barron 0-1; E Anders 0-1; L Washington 1-0;
           D Hightower 1-0   FIU – T Smith 1-0
TACKLES: UA – R McClain 6-4; D Hightower 3-3; M Barron 2-4; J Arenas 4-1;
           M Johnson 4; M Dareus 3-1; T Cody 2-1; K Jackson 2-1
           FIU – S Bryant 3-6; A Gaitor 7; A Parker 4-3; D Johnson 4-3; W Fraser 4-3;
           T Smith 3-2; J Cyprien 4; T Starling 3

1	2	3	4	5	6	7	8	9	10
FLORIDA	TEXAS	USC	ALABAMA	MISSISSIPPI	PENN STATE	BRIGHAM YOUNG	CALIFORNIA	LSU	BOISE STATE

The Kinks in Tide's Armor Can be Fixed

By RANDY KENNEDY

Alabama defensive lineman Marcell Dareus (57) celebrates his second-quarter sack of Florida International quarterback Paul McCall (12).

STAFF PHOTO/MARK ALMOND

There's no reason to overreact to a second straight week of Alabama displaying an inability to put away a team it's clearly dominating in every way except on the scoreboard.

Even after Saturday night's mostly uninspired 40-14 win over Florida International, Alabama is a solid top-5 team — and perhaps ever more entrenched near the top of the polls after Houston revealed Oklahoma State as a pretender.

But there's a difference between a very good team (which Alabama undoubtedly is) and a great team (the jury is most definitely still out on that). In the Crimson Tide's case, the difference is a shaky kick-off team that has allowed a touchdown return in two straight games and a secondary that is not always playing like a unit that receives the personal attention of the head coach every day.

Remember when Alabama fans were worried about having to break in a new quarterback behind a remade offensive line? A school-record 14 straight completions by junior Greg McElroy and a scoring average of 37 points per game through two games have all but erased those concerns.

But what has not gone away are the troubling breakdowns in the secondary that turned a 12-0 start into an 0-2 finish last season.

"I think we're a little out of sorts with the no-huddle," coach Nick Saban said at halftime Saturday night, though he could have just as easily been speaking at any time during last year's Sugar Bowl breakdown.

Florida International, a team that would probably go 1-7 against a full SEC schedule, had no production running the ball against Alabama and very little success throwing short passes against the Crimson Tide's speedy defense. Expect that trend to continue for Alabama, which is as athletic on defense as any team in the country.

But FIU quarterbacks Paul McCall and Wayne Younger had some success throwing the ball deep downfield to a receiver who appeared to be well covered, only to have the pass completed. Don't think every team on the Crimson Tide's schedule won't try the exact same approach.

It's not time for anyone to call for replacements in the secondary (although true freshman Dre Kirkpatrick is probably too talented to remain on the sidelines once he become more accustomed to the college game).

Despite that one glaring problem, Alabama still has a chance to be a special defense. Of course, we all knew that before the season started. What we didn't know was how quickly the offense would gel.

Even when injuries and sickness forced the Crimson Tide to play most of the night without stars Julio Jones, Roy Upchurch and Mark Ingram, Alabama gained yards in large chunks. In only his second game, freshman running back Trent Richardson began living up to all the hype surrounding him.

The bottom line is that, despite a couple of glitches, Saturday night did nothing to dampen Alabama's championship hopes.

Tightening the Screws

By BILL BRYANT

If it happens once, it's a freak occurrence. If it happens twice, it has a chance to become more than that.

A trend. A pattern.

And if it becomes a pattern, it can become a problem.

Particularly if you're a team that has BCS aspirations.

Fourth-ranked Alabama may have shrugged off a surprising first-half challenge by 33 1/2-point dog Florida International 40-14 on Saturday at Bryant-Denny Stadium, but it did not rid itself of the big-play bugaboo that plagued it in its opener against Virginia Tech.

And as the games this fall get progressively more difficult, and, by definition, more important, it would behoove the Crimson Tide to follow the words of the late actor John Houseman.

When it comes to picking up yardage and scoring points, make the opponents earn it.

"We have a lot of things we need to correct," Alabama coach Nick Saban said.

Kickoff coverage would be a good place to start. For the second straight week, the Crimson Tide allowed a long return for a touchdown.

It's not as if these guys aren't hustling. Most of these players are backups, looking to make a contribution wherever they can.

But too often this season, they're like a Labrador chasing a tennis ball on a tile floor. They sail right by it.

The Golden Panthers' T.Y. Hilton took a Leigh Tiffin kick at the 4-yard line and ran untouched into the south end zone. On his next kickoff, Tiffin endangered the cheerleaders with a boot out of bounds.

"Two weeks in a row where you give up a kickoff return for a touchdown and then we do the alternative kick and give up field position," Saban said. "That's something we need to improve on."

It's not limited to special teams, either. Two defensive breakdowns led to long touchdowns last week against Virginia Tech. On Saturday, the Crimson Tide let FIU slide early.

Facing a third-and-21 on its opening possession, Golden Panthers quarterback Paul McCall found Greg Ellingson, who beat Robby Green for a 46-yard completion. In the second quarter, Hilton scampered 25 yards on a slip screen - "I knew it was coming, I don't know how we didn't," Saban said. FIU soon went ahead 14-13 with the benefit of a pass interference penalty.

"Giving up a big play on third-and-long when they've got the ball on the 2-yard line ... we got a pass interference, which was big on a second-and-long," Saban said. "We allowed them to stay in the game with some mistakes."

In the second half, Alabama tightened the screws. Houdini had more breathing room in his underwater coffin than McCall had over the final two quarters (when he had just 54 yards passing). And in the end, in a game where the Crimson Tide was supposed to win big, they did.

But the energy that Saban requires was not evident for the full 60 minutes.

"I really wasn't happy with the enthusiasm our team came out and played with in the first half," he said. "The focus in games like this is to improve."

For Alabama to do that - and take aim at its lofty goals - it needs to continue to tighten the screws.

n. texas

Alabama running back Trent Richardson (3) escapes North Texas cornerback Royce Hill (21) and the rest of the North Texas defense in the second quarter.

CRIMSON TIDE **53**
MEAN GREEN **7**

09.19.09 | 11:20 a.m. | Bryant-Denny Stadium | Tuscaloosa, AL

Cranking It Up a Notch

By PAUl GATTIS

Class will go into session Monday and then Alabama will find out just how ugly a 53-7 win actually is.

You thought Alabama's smashing of North Texas looked good Saturday? Think again.

"Every game, you're going to learn and make mistakes and you're going to get better," tailback Mark Ingram said.

"We're going to watch the film on Monday, and although we had a lot of good things, there were some things we can learn from and that's where we'll get better."

So, just in case you were wondering, the fourth-ranked Crimson Tide is looking for another gear. Can a football team run on rocket fuel?

But being good and seeking to be better, maybe that's the difference between last year and this one. Maybe that's a team that's not only learning to win but learning to look for a higher level to ascend.

Now it's a matter of watching to see whether the Crimson Tide can reach it.

"It's never as easy as it looks," Tide safety Mark Barron said. "We just came out and played our responsibilities and everybody did the right thing today."

And when that happens, as it did Saturday, "That's the result," Barron said.

These may sound like standard responses from programmed players just reciting the script.

But this isn't like the Cinderella story of 2008. This is the product of three straight top-10 recruiting classes, two of them ranked No. 1.

These are players who know they are good and know how to push themselves to be better.

It's not just about posting the fastest stopwatch time or lifting the most weights on the benchpress.

"Our day was pretty good," cornerback/returner Javier Arenas said. "Improvement, to sum it up. I think we're going to get better from here on out."

Do you sense a theme?

"We're improving each week," Ingram said. "But I think as a team, we can be a lot better."

Alabama's talent is undeniable. And that talent pushed in a motivational frenzy are the ingredients of something special.

But now the season starts. Yes, the win over then-No. 7 Virginia Tech was nice, but that's so much history that the stat pages have started to yellow.

Alabama opens SEC play at home against Arkansas. That's SEC vs. SEC. That's big-boy football.

"It gets much tougher," quarterback Greg McElroy said. "Everything we've done to this point is all good and grand as far as getting the cobwebs out.

"Now it's time to really start playing. Our goal is to win an SEC championship. We need to continue to work and improve throughout the course of this week."

And the next. And the next.

"Just tuning up everything," Ingram said. "Run blocking, pass blocking, tackling, carrying the ball in the right hand. Just little things like that are going to make us better."

And perhaps even more special than last year's Tide.

ap top 10

released 09.20.09

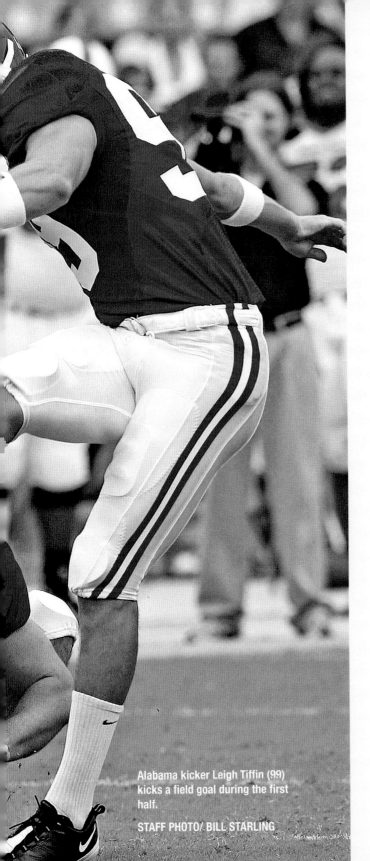

Alabama kicker Leigh Tiffin (99) kicks a field goal during the first half.

STAFF PHOTO/ BILL STARLING

TEAM	1ST	2ND	3RD	4TH	FINAL
ALABAMA	14	16	14	9	53
NORTH TEXAS	0	0	7	0	7

Attendance — 92,012 Bryant-Denny Stadium

SCORING SUMMARY

UA — G McElroy 2 yd run (L Tiffin kick), 13 plays, 95 yds, TOP 5:52
UA — M Maze 34 yd pass from G McElroy (L Tiffin kick), 6 plays, 67 yds, TOP 2:35
UA — T Richardson 1 yd run (L Tiffin kick), 5 plays, 83 yds, TOP 2:10
UA — M Ingram 29 yd pass from G McElroy (L Tiffin kick failed), 7 plays, 68 yds, TOP 3:25
UA — L Tiffin 35 yd field goal, 11 plays, 36 yards, TOP 2:08
UA — M Ingram 5 yd run (L Tiffin kick), 3 plays, 39 yds, TOP 0:54
UA — T Grant 1 yd run (L Tiffin kick), 6 plays, 33 yards, TOP 2:57
UNT — L Dunbar 34 yd pass from N Tune (J Knott kick), 5 plays, 78 yds, TOP 2:18
UA — L Tiffin 20 yd field goal, 11 plays, 37 yds, TOP 5:29
UA — T Grant 9 yd run (L Tiffin kick failed), 8 plays, 56 yds, TOP 3:43

TEAM STATISTICS

	UA	UNT
FIRST DOWNS	28	7
NET YARDS RUSHING	260	61
NET YARDS PASSING	263	126
COMPLETIONS-ATTEMPTS-INT	22-28-0	16-23-0
TOTAL OFFENSE YARDS	523	187
PENALTIES: NUMBER-YARDS	2-15	3-27
PUNTS-YARDS	1-49	9-379
PUNT RETURNS: NUMBER-YDS-TD	4-90-0	0-0-0
KICKOFF RETURNS: NUMBER-YDS-TD	2-71-0	7-119-0
POSSESSION TIME	30:43	29:17
SACKS BY: NUMBER-YARDS LOST	0-0	0-0
FIELD GOALS	2-2	0-0
FUMBLES: NUMBER-LOST	4-1	1-0

INDIVIDUAL OFFENSIVE STATISTICS

RUSHING: UA — M Ingram 8-91; T Richardson 11-87; T Grant 19-79; G McElroy 3-16; D Goode 1-14
UNT — J Hamilton 7-31; C Montgomery 7-8; J Mathis 4-7; N Tune 1-7; L Dunbar 5-5; D Carey 1-3; M Mosley 1-0

PASSING: UA — G McElroy 15-13-0, 176; S Jackson 13-9-0, 87
UNT — N Tune 23-16-0, 126

RECEIVING: UA — M Maze 4-49; M McCoy 3-38; M Ingram 3-38; T Grant 2-29; D Hanks 2-28; C Peek 2-26; B Smelley 2-13; B Gibson 1-21; E Alexander 1-11; M Bowman 1-7; T Richardson 1-3
UNT — D Carey 5-34; J Jackson 4-1; C Montgomery 3-17; L Dunbar 2-40; M Outlaw 2-34

INDIVIDUAL DEFENSIVE STATISTICS

INTERCEPTIONS: UA —None   UNT—None
SACKS: UA —None   UNT—None
TACKLES: UA — C Jordan 4-2; M Barron 3-2; T Cody 3-2; E Anders 2-3; R Green 2-3; N Johnson 3-1; J Arenas 2-1
UNT — D Cook 10-1; C Robertson 5-4; R Hill 6-2; A Adams 4-2; T Nwigwe 3-2; J Phillips 2-2; K Hill 2-2; D Williams 2-2; Ira Smith 2-1

1	2	3	4	5	6	7	8	9	10
FLORIDA	TEXAS	ALABAMA	MISSISSIPPI	PENN STATE	CALIFORNIA	LSU	BOISE STATE	MIAMI (FLA)	OKLAHOMA

Mal Moore's Legacy is Helping Tide Get Over Bear

By RAY MELICK

It was 10 years ago this month that the last "outsider" to sit in the athletics director's chair of the University of Alabama, Bob Bockrath, decided he'd had enough and resigned.

It was a move that would eventually bring in perhaps the ultimate "insider," Mal Moore.

Anyone who has followed Alabama football for the past 40 years knows how important the designations of "insider" and "outsider" are. In fact, Alabama football and Alabama football fans became a sort of national college football punch line among sports journalists and commentators who, while watching a parade of coaches go through Tuscaloosa, would shake their heads and say, "those people won't be happy until they find a way to bring back 'The Bear.'"

How ironic, then, that it took such an insider as Moore to break Alabama free of what seemed to be, at times, an unhealthy obsession with the past.

When you start to talk about Moore's legacy, that has to be at the top.

Moore untied the apron strings that some believed permanently connected "Mama" to the head coach's office when he replaced former Bryant player Mike DuBose with very non-Alabamian Dennis Franchione (although it could be argued Franchione was indeed a "family" hire, the candidate pushed by the Lee Roy Jordan-led Texas side of the Bryant "family" tree).

But Franchione was followed by Mike Price, who, if he had any connection to any of the power structure that surrounded Alabama athletics, didn't have a strong enough connection to help him when he needed it most.

While Moore reverted to "family" to clean up the Price fiasco by hiring former Alabama player Mike Shula, it was an act of desperation as much as anything. Shula never sought the job and by all accounts never thought of himself as a college football coach, a self-assessment that would prove accurate.

But when it came time to replace Shula, Moore was more than willing to put aside past rivalries in order to get the best coach, approaching Steve Spurrier and Rich Rodriguez before finally landing Nick Saban.

Forget capital campaigns, scholarships endowed, the success of nonfootball sports, even the run-ins with the NCAA that have occurred under Moore's watch. Moore's single greatest accomplishment as athletics director has to be finally getting Alabama fans to quit looking backward and start looking forward by bringing them Saban.

If contracts mean anything (a stretch, I know), Saban is set to be the head coach at Alabama for a long time. Will it be long enough to develop his own family tree of coaches? When Saban finally does go off to that great fishing hole in the mountains, will a new generation of Alabama fans clamor for someone with a Saban connection the way previous generations argued that no one deserved to coach football at Alabama who couldn't claim some direct link to The Bear?

Of course, if Saban left tomorrow, it could all blow up and bring Alabama fans right back to clamoring for "one of their own," someone who would be loyal to Alabama.

Oh, wait. They've already got that person. Mal Moore.

Alabama running back Terry Grant (29) tries to run past North Texas cornerback DaWaylon Cook (10) during the second half.

STAFF PHOTO/BILL STARLING

No Longer Overlooked

Carpenter, Tide's left tackle, was largely unrecruited out of high school

By DON KAUSLER, JR.

Because pass blocking was an undeveloped skill, because the Hephzibah Rebels run the Wing-T offense, and because grades were an issue, James Carpenter was largely ignored by college football recruiters during his senior year in high school.

But when you're largely large - Carpenter was 6-foot-5 and pushing the 300 pounds he weighs today - it's hard to be ignored.

Iowa State was the only large school that wanted Carpenter. It was coached by Gene Chizik. Yes, that Gene Chizik.

So Alabama's new left tackle knows Auburn's new coach well?

"Say what? Oh, yeah," Carpenter said.

And college football fans are getting to know the player who has taken the place of the 2008 Outland Trophy winner, the player who wasn't attracting attention from Alabama or other elite programs three years ago. Just Chizik.

Say what? Carpenter signed with Iowa State, but academic shortcomings led him to Coffeyville (Kan.) Community College.

Success was not instant.

"The first couple of games, he started a little slow," Jared Powers, Coffeyville's offensive line coach said. "The third game, it started to click. Once he got confident with the schemes, he took off. Then it was phenomenal. He'd be 50 yards downfield, blocking people - defensive ends, defensive backs. "

Suddenly, recruiters noticed.

"It was starting to get out of hand," Powers said. "Schools were here left and right, calling him, calling me."

Oklahoma led the parade. Alabama marched in.

"Coach (Joe) Pendry came here and said, 'I hear you've got this big ol' mountain of a guy,'" Powers recalled, referring to the Crimson Tide's offensive line coach.

Carpenter visited Oklahoma, Alabama, Iowa State, Ole Miss and Texas Tech.

"I wasn't sure which way James would go: closest to home or the one who recruited him the longest?" Powers said.

The opportunity to fill the big void left by departing left tackle Andre Smith was one attraction.

It wasn't the only reason he signed with Alabama.

"I always wanted to play in the SEC," Carpenter said. "Growing up, I liked Georgia."

He enrolled at Alabama in time to participate in spring practice. By last month, he was entrenched at the starting left tackle spot.

Following the Tide's 40-14 victory over Florida International, Alabama's coaching staff named Carpenter one of the Tide's offensive players of the week.

Football on this level is "way faster" than what Carpenter experienced in junior college. And, he said, "I've never worked hard like this, ever."

"It looks like he's developed another gear," Bowen said. "He was a late bloomer here. He's really matured and developed that killer instinct.

"Now if he keeps it up, it's going to pay off - literally. I told James his senior year, 'It's on you. You have the size. A lot of people can say, 'I didn't get a chance 'cause I ain't big enough.' You don't have that excuse. It's a matter of how bad you want it.'"

arkansas

Alabama defensive lineman Lorenzo Washington (97) blocks a third-quarter punt by Arkansas punter Dylan Breeding (14).

CRIMSON TIDE | 35
RAZORBACKS | 7

09.26.09 | 2:30 p.m. | Bryant-Denny Stadium | Tuscaloosa, AL

On This Day, Tide's Offense Second to None

By DON KAUSLER JR.

All the talk coming into Alabama's Southeastern Conference opener against Arkansas focused on the Tide's third-ranked defense clashing with the Razorbacks' second-ranked offense. Ryan Mallett this. Big plays that.

It turns out the Razorbacks had the second-best offense on the field.

"I stood up at the end of our meeting last night and said, 'You know what? I'm sick and tired or hearing about how Arkansas has such an explosive offense. We can be those guys, too,'" Alabama quarterback Greg McElroy said after the third-ranked Crimson Tide's 35-7 victory Saturday at Bryant-Denny Stadium.

"We went into this game with a chip on our shoulder and the guys made plays."

Big ones. Like an 80-yard touchdown pass, a 52-yard touchdown run and a 50-yard touchdown pass on a trick play. And enough little ones to put the game away with a 13-play, 99-yard touchdown drive.

"We want some respect, too," McElroy said, "and we got that today."

Alabama's defense had something to do with making Mallett and the Razorbacks (1-2) look inferior. The third-ranked Tide (4-0) held an offense that came in averaging 44.5 points and 538 yards to one touchdown and 254 yards. It held Mallett, a 6-foot-7 sophomore who set school records last week with 408 yards and five touchdown passes in a 52-41 loss to Georgia, to 12-of-35 passing and 160 yards.

McElroy completed 17-of-24 passes for 291 yards and three touchdowns. Good thing, because the nation's fifth-ranked rushing offense (267.7 yards per game) was held to 134 yards.

"They took away the run," McElroy said. "That's something we expected. We knew we'd have to make some plays in the air."

The Tide made plays, period.

Freshman running back Trent Richardson ran 52 yards for the Tide's first touchdown, breaking five tackles and dodging a would-be tackler at the goal line.

McElroy threw 50 yards to Julio Jones for the second touchdown on a trick play. "Wildcat North Sweep Reverse Pass," said running back Mark Ingram, who took the direct snap in the Wildcat formation. He handed off on a reverse to running back Terry Grant, who flipped to McElroy. Jones was all alone at the 16-yard line. "I just didn't want to overthrow him," McElroy said.

After Arkansas scored to make it 14-7 with 10:45 left in the first

Alabama wide receiver Darius Hanks (15) goes high to catch a pass over Arkansas strong safety Jerico Nelson (31) in the third quarter.

STAFF PHOTO/ MARK ALMOND

ap top 10 released 09.27.09

TEAM	1ST	2ND	3RD	4TH	FINAL
ALABAMA	0	14	14	7	35
ARKANSAS	0	0	7	0	7

Attendance   92,012 Bryant-Denny Stadium

SCORING SUMMARY

UA   T Richardson 52 yd run (L Tiffin kick), 6 plays, 86 yds, TOP 3:14
UA   J Jones 50 yd pass from G McElroy (L Tiffin kick), 1 play, 50 yds, TOP 0:10
AR   G Childs 18 yd pass from R Mallett (A Tejada kick), 5 plays, 55 yds, TOP 2:17
UA   M Maze 80 yd pass from G McElroy (L Tiffin kick), 1 play, 80 yds, TOP 0:20
UA   M Ingram 14 yd pass from G McElroy (L Tiffin kick), 5 plays, 35 yds, TOP 2:28
UA   M Ingram 2 yd run (L Tiffin kick), 13 plays, 99 yds, TOP 6:28

TEAM STATISTICS

	UA	AR
FIRST DOWNS	18	14
NET YARDS RUSHING	134	63
NET YARDS PASSING	291	191
COMPLETIONS-ATTEMPTS-INT	17-24-0	16-41-1
TOTAL OFFENSE YARDS	425	254
PENALTIES: NUMBER-YARDS	7-60	11-98
PUNTS-YARDS	7-288	10-358
PUNT RETURNS: NUMBER-YDS-TD	5-75-0	1-3-0
KICKOFF RETURNS: NUMBER-YDS-TD	2-33-0	4-102-0
POSSESSION TIME	33:36	26:24
SACKS BY: NUMBER-YARDS LOST	3-28	1-2
FIELD GOALS	0-0	0-0
FUMBLES: NUMBER-LOST	0-0	0-0

INDIVIDUAL OFFENSIVE STATISTICS

RUSHING: UA – T Richardson 9-65; M Ingram 17-50; T Grant 13-16; G McElroy 2-3;
              AR – M Smith 12-61; R Wingo 4-12; B Green 2-10; K Davis 2-6;
              D Johnson 2-1; D Breeding 1-1; R Mallett 3-(-28)
PASSING: UA – G McElroy 24-17-0, 291
              AR – R Mallett 35-12-1, 160; T Wilson 6-4-0, 31
RECEIVING: UA – R Upchurch 3-30; M Ingram 3-21; M Maze 2-88; J Jones 2-65;
              C Peek 2-19; T Richardson 2-16; D Hanks 1-32; T Grant 1-18; P Dial 1-2
              AR – J Adams 6-81; G Childs 4-60; D Williams 2-26; J Wright 1-14
              B Green 1-8; C Hamilton 1-3; K Davis 1-(-1)

INDIVIDUAL DEFENSIVE STATISTICS

INTERCEPTIONS: UA – J Woodall 1-24   AR – None
SACKS: UA – J Arenas 2-0; E Anders 1-0   AR – A Davis 1-0
TACKLES: UA – Mark Barron 2-5; J Arenas 4-1; R McClain 4-1; K Jackson 2-3;
              J Woodall 3-1; E Anders 3-0; C Rogers 2-1; C Reamer 2-1; A Sharrief 2-1;
              M Dareus 2-0; AR – J Franklin 5-5; A Davis 5-2; M Harris 3-4;
              T Wright 3-2; J Bequette 2-3; J Nelson 2-2; W Davis 2-2

1	2	3	4	5	6	7	8	9	10
FLORIDA	TEXAS	ALABAMA	LSU	BOISE STATE	VIRGINIA TECH	USC	OKLAHOMA	OHIO STATE	CINCINNATI

(l-r)Alabama linebacker Rolando McClain (25), defensive lineman Marcell Dareus (57), defensive lineman Terrence Cody (62) and linebacker Dont'a Hightower (30) celebrate the tackle of Arkansas tailback Michael Smith (21) in the first quarter.

STAFF PHOTO/ MARK ALMOND

half, McElroy came back on the very next play to throw an 80-yard touchdown pass to Marquis Maze.

"We watched film of those guys," Maze said. "We knew we had a shot of making big plays. Their corners were kind of slow. They rolled the coverage over to Julio and left me one-on-one. It was a stutter, stop and go. Once I saw him bite on the stop, I just ran past him and made a play."

Ingram scored the last two touchdowns, on a 14-yard pass and a 2-yard run. That last score capped a 13-play, 99-yard drive.

"That drive was huge," Ingram said. "That just shows a lot about the character of our offense."

Lots of little plays added up for the big-play offense.

"It was kind of a pivotal moment in the game," McElroy said of the drive that started at the 1-yard line with 4:40 left in the third quarter and Alabama leading 28-7.

"Any time you're backed up, that's a momentum shift in their favor," McElroy said. "The goal coming out in a situation like that is to get a first down. You get a first down, that changes the momentum. … The fact we went 99 yards is a real tribute to our offensive line, and our wide receivers and running backs and our play calling."

But the Tide's defense should not be overshadowed. Despite losing standout sophomore linebacker Dont'a Hightower to what appeared to be a serious knee injury late in a scoreless first quarter, Alabama allowed the potent Razorbacks to convert only two-of-14 third-down plays.

"To hold those guys to seven points was really good," Alabama coach Nick Saban said. "It was a total team effort.

"Some of the things we did today were not conventional. We tried to play Cover 2 and rush the inside backers and do some things different. … We played a little more zone today than we normally would."

The Tide went with five and sometimes six defensive backs. Senior cornerback Javier Arenas blitzed twice in the second quarter and sacked Mallett.

Still, this day belonged to an Alabama offense that was determined to make more big plays than that other offense.

"We've got a group of wide receivers and running backs that are as explosive as any group in the country," McElroy said. "I feel very strongly about that and their ability to make plays."

The Tide's actions spoke louder than words.

Hard to Match LB's Versatility, Emotion

By MARK McCARTER

When Dont'a Hightower crashed to the earth in a heap, there was an almost immediate sense of trepidation. Watch the replay, watch the landing, you had a sense right then he was going from a spot on the Alabama depth chart to a spot on an orthopedist's schedule.

When Dont'a Hightower crashed, so did fellow linebacker Rolando McClain.

"When it happened on the field, I didn't want to believe," McClain said. "When he went down, I kinda went down and squatted. I hate it for him.

"He's not just my teammate, he's like a little brother," McClain continued. "When he went out, it was like a part of me went out."

Alabama didn't merely lose a linebacker for the season when the sophomore Hightower tore ligaments in his left knee in Saturday's win over Arkansas. It lost an intangible quality Hightower brought to the defense. It's not merely a physical loss. Said Javier Arenas, "Emotionally, I think it will be tough" replacing Hightower.

"It's going to be hard for me to get over it," said McClain on Monday.

This isn't like getting a pawn captured in chess. This was like losing the queen three moves into the game. Hightower is one of the players Alabama could least afford to lose.

"When you miss a player like Dont'a, he's an incredible player," defensive end Lorenzo Washington said. "You don't want to say 'irreplaceable,' but his emotional leadership and being out there, he's a dominating player."

The injury, Washington said, motivated him and his teammates to "want to get back there and keep hitting."

There is surely some chatter on the message boards about the legality of the block, or whether it was a cheap shot. It was perfectly legal. It was, to borrow from the NASCAR phrase that explains nine-tenths of all racing wrecks, "just one of them football deals."

It's what will happen when big, fast, strong people hurl their bodies at each other at awkward angles. It's what will happen because, upon inventing football, God didn't make human ligaments from the same material as suspension bridge cables.

That Alabama fortunately avoided a bunch of "them football deals" last season was important in its unbeaten regular season.

With Julio Jones having missed most of two games, with Roy Upchurch still not full speed

and now Hightower gone, Alabama has suffered more significant injuries in this short season than all of last year.

In his characteristic optimism, coach Nick Saban looks at the loss of Hightower as "opportunity it creates for somebody else to go in and take advantage of reacting to what has happened. Of course, were an earthquake to send California sinking into the Pacific, Saban would note that "it presents an opportunity for people in Phoenix to have beach houses."

With the exception of Arenas, Hightower was probably the most versatile man on the team, a terrific inside linebacker who was a devastating pass rusher. It'll be a committee of replacements taking over for him.

"There's not one guy who can replace him right now," McClain said.

Trouble with a committee, there are still only 11 players allowed on the field. Hightower was two or three players all by himself.

kentucky

Alabama linebacker Courtney Upshaw
(41) grabs a fumble after Alabama
linebacker Rolando McClain (25) hits
Kentucky tailback Derrick Locke (20) in
the second quarter.

STAFF PHOTO/MARK ALMOND

CRIMSON TIDE | 38
WILDCATS | 20

10.03.09 | 11:20 a.m. | Commonwealth Stadium | Lexington, KY

By RAY MELICK

One Internet headline Sunday described the changes in the latest AP Top 25 as a "rash," and that was as good a description as any for the plague that has infected college football this year.

Look at how the mighty have fallen just this past weekend: California fell 18 spots, from No. 6 to No. 24; Ole Miss fell from No. 4 to No. 21; Penn State dropped 10 spots after losing to Iowa; even Miami, which made a meteoric climb up the polls the first three weeks, dropped eight places after losing to Virginia Tech.

LSU barely escaped Mississippi State. And now even Florida fans are worrying after seeing Tim Tebow carted off to a hospital with a concussion.

Just how long will doctors keep Tebow out?

In the NFL, doctors have been known to keep a player who has suffered a concussion on the sidelines from three weeks to a month. Florida has LSU in two weeks. And in each of the past three years, the winner of the Florida-LSU game has gone on to win the BCS National Championship.

But one top team that just hasn't had a bad week is Alabama. A month into the season, the Crimson Tide is making a case for No. 1. Not only is the Tide winning in impressive fashion, but so is Virginia Tech, the team Alabama beat in the opener. And every Hokie win makes Alabama's resume that much stronger with pollsters and computers.

At quarterback, Greg McElroy is doing more than these same Tide coaches ever let his predecessor at quarterback, John Parker Wilson, do.

With no Andre Smith or Antoine Caldwell, the line is not as straight-ahead powerful as last year. But it is more athletic, with all five positions, including the center, used in pulling situations. Throw nose guard Terrence Cody in at fullback and you've got an Andre Smith-style lead blocker for short-yardage situations.

But what impresses other coaches, in particular, is what the Tide is doing defensively with some of its key personnel.

On one play Alabama can appear to be in a 3-2 front (three down linemen and two linebackers), only to have one of those linebackers suddenly become a defensive end and then it's a 4-2. Sometimes safety Mark Barron or cornerback Javier Arenas will come up on the outside like a linebacker and, just as suddenly a 3-2 becomes a 4-3, all without changing personnel.

That will fry an offensive coordinator's headset.

Before Dont'a Hightower's injury, Alabama would sometimes line up in a four man front, only to have Hightower stand up and drop into pass coverage and suddenly it's a three-man rush with eight playing pass protection. Or Hightower would stand up and drop into coverage and either Rolando McClain or Arenas or Barron would suddenly produce pass rush pressure from another direction.

That kind of confusion will cause quarterbacks to yell at their offensive linemen.

It's fun to watch, if you like defensive football, because it creates havoc with offensive calls that try to anticipate defensive schemes based on alignment and changing personnel.

It will be interesting to see how the loss of Hightower changes what Alabama has been doing.

Because right now, no one can be sure what Alabama is doing on any given play.

That's what happens when a team is playing like it can do it all.

Alabama... playing like a team that can do it all

(38)John Conner gets tackled by (28) Javier Arenas and (32) Eryk Anders in the 2nd quarter.

STAFF PHOTO/ MICHAEL MERCIER

ap top 10 released 10.04.09

TEAM	1ST	2ND	3RD	4TH	FINAL
ALABAMA	7	14	17	0	38
KENTUCKY	6	0	7	7	20

Attendance   70,967   Commonwealth Stadium

SCORING SUMMARY

UA   M Ingram 11 yd run (L Tiffin kick), 3 plays, 37 yds, TOP 0:57
UK   L Seiber 49 yd field goal, 10 plays, 36 yds, TOP 4:36
UK   L Seiber 49 yd field goal, 14 plays, 38 yds, TOP 5:28
UA   C Peek 3 yd pass from G McElroy (L Tiffin kick), 13 plays, 97 yds, TOP 6:50
UA   C Upshaw 45 yd fumble recovery (L Tiffin kick)
UA   M Ingram 32 yd run (L Tiffin kick), 2 plays, 38 yds, TOP 0:45
UA   L Tiffin 36 yd field goal, 6 plays, 29 yds, TOP 2:17
UK   R Cobb 45 yd pass from M Hartline (L Seiber kick), 3 plays, 55 yds, TOP 0:34
UA   D Hanks 7 yd pass from G McElroy (L Tiffin kick), 13 plays, 76 yards, TOP 5:44
UK   A Smith 2 yd run (L Seiber kick), 16 plays, 65 yds, TOP 5:47

TEAM STATISTICS

TEAM STATISTICS	UA	UK
FIRST DOWNS	18	20
NET YARDS RUSHING	204	133
NET YARDS PASSING	148	168
COMPLETIONS-ATTEMPTS-INT	15-26-0	17-32-3
TOTAL OFFENSE YARDS	352	301
PENALTIES: NUMBER-YARDS	6-47	7-78
PUNTS-YARDS	5-199	3-116
PUNT RETURNS: NUMBER-YDS-TD	0-0-0	4-58-0
KICKOFF RETURNS: NUMBER-YDS-TD	5-141-0	5-126-0
POSSESSION TIME	33:36	26:24
SACKS BY: NUMBER-YARDS LOST	2-10	1-2
FIELD GOALS	1-1	2-2
FUMBLES: NUMBER-LOST	0-0	1-1

INDIVIDUAL OFFENSIVE STATISTICS

RUSHING: UA – M Ingram 22-140; T Richardson 14-26; P Fitzgerald 1-17;
           R Upchurch 1-13; G McElroy 3-5; M Maze 1-3
          UK – D Locke 20-75; A Smith 5-28; R Cobb 4-21; M Allen 4-7;
           J Conner 1-3
PASSING: UA – G McElroy 26-15-0, 148
          UK – M Hartline 31-17-3, 168; R Cobb 1-0-0, 0
RECEIVING: UA – C Peek 6-65; D Hanks 2-34; J Jones 2-13; R Upchurch 2-0;
           E Alexander 1-21; T Richardson 1-9; M Ingram 1-6
          UK – D Locke 6-63; R Cobb 3-57; K Lanxter 3-26; M Allen 3-12;
           C Matthews 1-8; J Conner 1-2

INDIVIDUAL DEFENSIVE STATISTICS

INTERCEPTIONS: UA – R McClain 1-21; M Barron 1-6; E Anders 1-0   UK – None
SACKS: UA – E Anders 1-0; C Upshaw 1-0;   UK – D Evans 1-0
TACKLES: UA – R McClain 8-4; M Barron 6-2; J Arenas 5-3; C Reamer 5-1;
          M Dareus 4-1; C Upshaw 4-0; J Woodall 3-0; E Anders 2-1
          UK – D Trevathan 5-5; M Johnson 2-8; C Harrison 5-2; C Burden 2-3;
          W Guy 1-4; M Neloms 3-1; R Lumpkin 3-1; S Maxwell 2-2

1	2	3	4	5	6	7	8	9	10
FLORIDA	TEXAS	ALABAMA	LSU	VIRGINIA TECH	BOISE STATE	USC	CINCINNATI	OHIO STATE	TCU

Kentucky defenders close in on Alabama wide receiver Julio Jones (8) on a second-quarter pass play.

STAFF PHOTO/MARK ALMOND

Into the Blue

By MARK McCARTER

The instant that Florida wrapped up its 34-point win over Kentucky a week ago, fairly or not, an extra burden got dumped on top of Alabama.

Now, show us what you've got.

Through a quirk of scheduling the Wildcats played No. 1 Florida and No. 3 Alabama on back-to-back weeks. We live in a world where we must compare - Burger King or McDonalds? Fox News or CNN? Ginger or Mary Ann? - and this left us with the perfect lens to do so.

After Florida shelled Kentucky 41-7, Alabama beat Kentucky 38-20 Saturday afternoon.

"Alabama, defensively, is just as good as Florida, (might) be better," said Kentucky coach Rich Brooks, in the role of a cartoon character who fell off a cliff, then had an anvil conk him in the noggin.

"Offensively, they're a totally different style," Brooks said of the Tide. "They're a great football team and I'd expect we'll be seeing those teams in the conference championship game."

Comparative scores are as meaningless as a campaign speech. But not if you're a voter two time zones away who sees nothing but an 18-point margin. With Florida and Texas both taking the weekend off, this put Alabama squarely in the national focus.

"They're both really good teams," said Kentucky linebacker Micah Johnson. "They are the No. 1 and No. 3 teams in the nation. This week, we actually played with them and had a chance to win, but we killed ourself."

You want to use this for how Alabama looks in comparison to Florida?

A better idea: Use it for how Alabama looks in the mirror.

Not as Good as Gators?

Tide good enough to beat Wildcats

By DON KAUSLER JR.

Alabama was dressed in its sparkling white road uniforms. Kentucky came nearly head to toe in glistening blue.

But what about that other team on the Commonwealth Stadium field? Orange you the Florida Gators?

If people squinted, they might have seen the ghosts of the nation's top-ranked team, lingering after their 41-7 victory over Kentucky the previous week.

Now that third-ranked Alabama (5-0, 2-0 in the Southeastern Conference) won one game Saturday, defeating the Wildcats 38-20 in workmanlike fashion, let the other big, fun game begin.

Who's No. 1?

Kentucky (2-2, 0-2) should qualify as the judge and jury to issue an opinion in a matter that might not be settled until Dec. 5, if or when Alabama and Florida meet in the Southeastern Conference championship game.

"I think Alabama defensively is just as good as Florida," said Kentucky coach Rich Brooks, whose Wildcats had 20 first downs and 301 yards Saturday compared to 11 first downs and 179 total yards a week ago.

"They offensively are a totally different style. … They're a great football team. I expect we'll be seeing both of those teams playing in the conference championship game."

Kentucky safety Winston Guy was a little less diplomatic.

"Florida's a more speed, finesse team. Alabama's more powerful," he said.

"We're not really worried about Florida," said standout middle linebacker Rolando McClain, who forced a key fumble and had one of the Tide's three interceptions. "They're Florida. We're Alabama. You can't compare us and them."

The Tide merely worried about beating Kentucky, and for most of the first half, there was much to worry about.

Alabama scored 57 seconds into the game on an 11-yard run by Mark Ingram. Florida led 31-0 after one quarter a week ago. Here came the Tide. And here came the comparisons.

But the first quarter ended with Alabama leading 7-6, and Kentucky had edges in first downs (8-2), plays (26-9), total yards (81-26) and time of possession (12 minutes to 3). So much for the comparisons.

The Wildcats had forced four consecutive three-and-outs, and they were aiming for a fifth after pinning Alabama at its own 3-yard line.

On first down, freshman running back Trent Richardson was hit by Kentucky linebacker Micah Johnson at the goal line. Richardson went down in the end zone, but officials marked his forward progress at the 1-foot line.

Perhaps never has a 2-yard loss been such a key offensive play.

"It was huge," said Ingram, who ran 22 times for 140 yards and two touchdowns. "I thought it was a safety. Trent got out by a half inch."

But Alabama still was in danger of another three-and-out before Greg McElroy threw 21 yards over the middle to tight end Colin Peek on a third-and-7 play.

"That was a big breath of air right there," Alabama senior right tackle Drew Davis said.

McElroy completed three more third-down passes, the last a 3-yard TD pass to Peek that gave Alabama a 14-6 lead with 40 seconds left in the quarter. It looked as if that would be the halftime score.

But McClain knocked the ball loose from Kentucky running back Derrick Locke on the next play from scrimmage. Linebacker Courtney Upshaw, making his first start, caught the fumble in midair and raced 45 yards for a touchdown with 20 seconds left in the first half, scoring only 19 seconds after the previous touchdown.

"We were pleased with one touchdown," McElroy said. "That's all we expected. To get two like that was gravy. It was a huge swing and really killed their momentum going in at the half."

So instead of Kentucky leading 8-7 after a possible safety, Alabama led 21-6 at halftime.

"That was the real killer," Brooks said.

The Tide led by as many as 25 in the second half but gave up two touchdowns that ultimately will matter only to people determined to compared Alabama to Florida.

The Wildcats knocked out Tebow, Florida's star senior quarterback, sending the 2007 Heisman Trophy winner to the hospital with a concussion.

Alabama came out of Saturday's game unscathed physically, but the Tide's mettle was tested by the Gators, er, Wildcats.

"It's a win and we'll take the win," said linebacker Rolando McClain. "We're not really satisfied with it. We know we can play a lot better. (We've got to) try to get better, get ready for Ole Miss."

This was a glorious blue-sky day, reminding us that college football is best served in open air and in daylight. An enthusiastic crowd filled Commonwealth Stadium, though it should be noted the day's loudest ovation was reserved for the first-quarter introduction of the UK basketball team, at which point Alabama was doing its darndest to keep things close.

But, as often happens to the downtrodden in college football, these Wildcats found a black cloud and hunkered down under it. Kentucky blew two coverages in a 97-yard Alabama drive, then immediately fumbled away a 45-yard defensive touchdown by Courtney Upshaw on the last play of the half. Add two more UK turnovers in its first six plays of the second half and next thing you know, it's Alabama 31, Kentucky 6, at the 10:10 mark in the third. Game, set, match.

Let the record show, Florida rang up 31 points in the first 15 minutes.

Despite the win, surely this marked the end of the Heisman Trophy candidacy of Greg McElroy, which was no more substantive than whipped cream anyway. He seems like a nice kid and he's a capable quarterback. But it was less sudden national groundswell and more a peculiar creation of someone scouring for a different story angle to put him on some "watch list."

"G-Mac is a great quarterback," receiver Darius Hanks said and indeed he hit some clutch passes, notably a pair of third-down-converting lasers on that 97-yard touchdown drive. But 15-for-26 for 148 yards doesn't get the network bobbleheads' endorsements.

That brings us to one last Florabama comparison. The Heisman front-runner, one Timothy Richard Tebow, was hauled groggily away from this stadium last weekend, barfing in an ambulance, the victim of a concussion.

Sure, you like Florida's margin of victory. But you gotta like McElroy's exit a lot better.

ole mis

Alabama linebacker Cory Reamer (13) strips the ball from Ole Miss wide receiver Dexter McCluster (22) on a third-quarter punt return. Reamer recovered the fumble.

STAFF PHOTO/MARK ALMOND

CRIMSON TIDE | 22
REBELS | 3

10.10.09 | 2:30 p.m. | Vaught-Hemingway Stadium | Oxford, MS

Rebels But a Speed Bump for Bama

By MARK McCARTER

Six o'clock, straight up, and Nick Saban jogged off the field. In a stadium almost otherwise devoid of life, thousands of Alabama fans in a wedge of crimson rose to applaud and sing his praises.

Saban looked up, smiled and waved an index finger, straight up.

So much was yet to unfold and so much had already unraveled on this monumental day of college football. Still, Saban might have made a valid point to display the universal "We're No. 1" sign.

Alabama is 6-0. One of the biggest hurdles it had anticipated was little more than a speed bump. The Tide cleared Ole Miss with ease, 22-3.

Meanwhile, as the evening rolled on, life wouldn't be easy for Florida, the consensus No. 1. The Gators held off LSU in Baton Rouge 13-3.

While Alabama remained unbeaten, moments before kickoff here, Auburn's perfect season officially went unperfect. The 17th-ranked Tigers failed to score in the first quarter for the first time all season, got themselves caught in an avalanche and lost to Arkansas 44-23.

The road wasn't kind to Alabama A&M, either. The Bulldogs, oh-for-forever at Grambling, lost to the Tigers 41-20.

Once upon a time, this game was circled on the calendar. In this corner, Ole Miss, the upstart team on a rise, winner of six in a row to finish the '08 season. In the other, Alabama, back in its traditional role of national power.

Heck, Saban even admitted that "we worked on these guys in spring practice."

Instead, it was something of a letdown, like a much-anticipated Christmas where Santa Claus decided to rely more heavily on the products of Fruit of the Loom rather than Mattel.

Ole Miss was woeful on offense. The red zone was dead zone for the Alabama offense, which had to settle for five Leigh Tiffin field goals.

Still, with a dominating performance that Saban called "probably the most complete team win we've had all year, in a difficult situation," to nitpick on the dearth of touchdowns is to gripe that your new Ferrari doesn't have enough cup holders.

The Alabama defense was again phenomenal. Poor Jevan Snead, the Ole Miss quarterback, who found himself being booed by the home crowd. He completed only 11 of 34 passes and was constantly pressured by the Alabama defense.

Finally, we can put to rest some hype. Ole Miss is a movie where the trailers are terrific, but when you go to the theater it turns out to be just another dreary, predictable romantic comedy that's as funny as a knock-knock joke.

ap top 10
released 10.11.09

TEAM	1ST	2ND	3RD	4TH	FINAL
ALABAMA	3	13	3	3	38
OLE MISS	0	0	3	0	20

Attendance   62,657 Vaught-Hemingway Stadium

SCORING SUMMARY

UA   L Tiffin 25 yd field goal, 12 plays, 58 yds, TOP 4:01
UA   L Tiffin 21 yd field goal, 7 plays, 22 yds, TOP 2:27
UA   L Tiffin 22 yd field goal, 4 plays, 1 yd, TOP 1:00
UA   M Ingram 36 yd run (L Tiffin kick), 6 plays, 61 yds, TOP 2:49
UM   J Shene 25 yd field goal, 10 plays, 60 yds, TOP 4:02
UA   L Tiffin 21 yd field goal, 9 plays, 36 yds, TOP 4:49
UA   L Tiffin 31 yd field goal, 4 plays, 8 yds, TOP 2:08

TEAM STATISTICS

TEAM STATISTICS	UA	UM
FIRST DOWNS	17	12
NET YARDS RUSHING	200	57
NET YARDS PASSING	154	140
COMPLETIONS-ATTEMPTS-INT	16-35-0	11-34-4
TOTAL OFFENSE YARDS	354	197
PENALTIES: NUMBER-YARDS	4-30	4-16
PUNTS-YARDS	6-245	6-228
PUNT RETURNS: NUMBER-YDS-TD	3-5-0	3-32-0
KICKOFF RETURNS: NUMBER-YDS-TD	2-40-0	6-149-0
POSSESSION TIME	38:19	21:41
SACKS BY: NUMBER-YARDS LOST	1-15	2-14
FIELD GOALS	5-5	1-1
FUMBLES: NUMBER-LOST	2-1	3-1

INDIVIDUAL OFFENSIVE STATISTICS

RUSHING: UA — M Ingram 28-172; T Richardson 9-40
           UM — J Snead 5-29; D McCluster 6-15; B Bolden 10-11; E Davis 2-7
PASSING: UA — G McElroy 34-15-0, 147; P Fitzgerald 1-1-0, 7
           UM — J Snead 34-11-4, 140
RECEIVING: UA — M Maze 4-48; J Jones 4-42; C Peek 3-32; M Ingram 3-16;
           T Richardson 1-9; M Barron 1-7
           UM — B Bolden 4-76; D McCluster 3-22; S Hodge 2-21; M Summers 1-13;
           L Breaux 1-8

INDIVIDUAL DEFENSIVE STATISTICS

INTERCEPTIONS: UA — K Jackson 1-79; J Woodall 1-0; R McClain 1-0; J Arenas 1-0
           UM — None
SACKS: UA — E Anders 1-0   UM — J Cornell 0-1; G Hardy 1-0; K Lockett 0-1
TACKLES: UA — R McClain 4-3; J Arenas 4-1; C Reamer 4-0; K Jackson 4-0;
           M Barron 3-1; J Woodall 3-1
           UM — J Brown 7-3; J Cornell 5-2; K Lewis 4-3; P Trahan 3-4; A Walker 2-4;
           K Lockett 1-4; J McGee 3-1; L Brumfield 2-2

Alabama running back Mark Ingram (22) flies as Alabama tight end Preston Dial (85) blocks Ole Miss safety Johnny Brown (20).

STAFF PHOTO/MARK ALMOND

1	2	3	4	5	6	7	8	9	10
FLORIDA	ALABAMA	TEXAS	VIRGINIA TECH	BOISE STATE	USC	OHIO STATE	CINCINNATI	MIAMI FLORIDA	LSU

Alabama defensive lineman Terrence Cody (62) pressures
Mississippi quarterback Jevan Snead (4).

STAFF PHOTO/ROBIN CONN

Meanwhile, the Texas Longhorns, the nation's second-ranked team, spotted Colorado a 14-3 lead and then promptly ran off 35 unanswered points.

Still, Alabama has a legit claim to at least be in that "We're No. 1" conversation.

"You've got to be careful with your confidence," offensive tackle Mike Johnson said. "We're a confident group of guys. We know we should beat most teams we play. But at the same time, you've got to be able to prepare hard every week."

To that end, the man bold enough to lift that index finger would later use it to make a point.

"We've got a good team," Saban said. "The guys play hard. They play well together. There's a lot of things we can improve on. The key to the drill is, can we stay focused on the things we need to do, to improve, to be as good as we can be.

"So far," he said, "our team has answered every challenge. (But) this is like climbing a mountain. The higher you get, the more treacherous it gets."

Cold, Ruthless, Relentless

By PAUL GATTIS

This was cold. This was ruthless. This was relentless.

This was a 22-3 win that could not have been more convincing as a 50-0 blowout.

Alabama pounded Ole Miss without conscience, without regard to the largest crowd in stadium history, without concern for the growing notion that the Crimson Tide may indeed be the nation's best.

Do not be fooled by the score. Do not think Alabama is vulnerable.

Alabama, in football terms, killed Ole Miss on Saturday. To have done it by a more lopsided score would have been overkill.

And once was enough.

"We just play our ball," defensive tackle Terrence Cody said. "We don't showboat. We just go out, execute and play our game."

Name your score and it would have been a misnomer. Alabama 22, Ole Miss 3 was dominating, suffocating and captivating.

Even Alabama coach Nick Saban, Mr. Gloomy himself, did everything but bring a thesaurus to his postgame press conference to heap praise on his team.

"We really competed for 60 minutes in the game," Saban said. "We played hard, played physical. Everybody sold out for the team. That's great."

More Saban: "Great effort. Man, I can't tell you how proud I am of the effort and the toughness and the competitive character that our players showed in this game."

Remember that the Rebels once had a cause. They once were ranked No. 4 in the nation, once charmed more than one genius into thinking they could win the SEC West.

But the Crimson Tide stormed into Vaught-Hemingway Stadium and reminded Ole Miss who is boss.

Ole Miss scored its fewest points in a game since the dreary days of Ed Orgeron during the 0-8 SEC season of 2007. Ole Miss had 19 yards on 22 plays in the first half. Ole Miss quarterback Jevan Snead threw four interceptions.

"This was probably the most complete team win we've had this year in a difficult situation," Saban said.

This was a chilling performance on a chilly day, despite its imperfections.

"We've always got to get better," linebacker Rolando McClain said. "I never feel satisfied with what I do. I don't think my teammates do. I think they've bought into it, that we can always get better."

Line 'em up and Alabama will knock 'em down: South Carolina, Tennessee, LSU, Mississippi State, Chattanooga, Auburn.

Only Alabama, it appears, can stop Alabama at this point - no matter what confidence the benign score of 22-3 may falsely feed to the rest of the SEC.

"We ain't worried about the score," McClain said. "As a defense, we're just out there trying to stop the offense and I think that's what we did. "

A flaw? The offense failed to score a touchdown on five trips inside the Ole Miss 20.

"Unacceptable," tailback Mark Ingram said.

And self-awareness is why Alabama is a cold, ruthless, relentless team.

"The key to the drill is, Can we stay focused on doing the things we need to do to improve to be as good as we can be and not get complacent?" Saban said. "That's the key to the drill."

And the key to drilling one team after another.

Because, at this point, evidence screams only Alabama can stop Alabama.

Ole Miss linebacker Joel Kight (49) grabs Alabama defensive back Mark Barron (4) after a first-down on a fake punt in the first quarter.

STAFF PHOTO/MARK ALMOND

s. carolina

Alabama tight end Colin Peek (84) catches a third-quarter pass over South Carolina defensive end Cliff Matthews (83).

STAFF PHOTO/MARK ALMOND

CRIMSON TIDE
GAMECOCKS

10.17.09 | 6:45

20

6

uscaloosa, AL

Just Pretty Enough,

To Ease Into Top Billing!

By RANDY KENNEDY

It may not have looked that great, perhaps didn't even feel that great, to the Bama Nation. But there's a lot to be said for Alabama's 20-6 victory over South Carolina Saturday night.

That includes the notion that Alabama is No. 1.

Based on its play to this point in the season, the results of another wacky day in college football and just the feeling one gets when watching the Crimson Tide play, it has made a legitimate claim to the top spot in the polls and its timing couldn't have been better: the first BCS poll of the year will be released today.

No, it wasn't a pretty win, but it was an important win.

When Mark Barron produced a quick 7-0 lead thanks to his 77-yard interception return for a touchdown, it was difficult not to believe the Crimson Tide was primed to put away the Gamecocks early. That wasn't the case.

The offense — other than fabulous running back Mark Ingram, who supplied 246 rushing yards and a touchdown on 24 carries — struggled to establish itself and quarterback Greg McElroy has enjoyed better performances.

But it did enough, especially late when it needed a touchdown to close the matter.

The defense, as has been the case all season, was strong. When it appeared South Carolina might get something going offensively, the Crimson Tide defense would make a key stop.

In the first quarter, Alabama put the Gamecocks in second down-and-25, fourth-and-27, second-and-20, fourth-and-22; in the second quarter, third-and-21 and second-and-16.

The luxury of Alabama's offense is the insurance its defense provides. Together, they produce a team that's pretty darn good. And right now, it may be the best team in the country.

It's not easy being the best or even among that number. Saturday's games proved that:

No. 1-ranked Florida needed a late field goal to beat Arkansas, the same Arkansas team Alabama slapped 35-7. It wasn't a win for the ages, but it was a win.

No. 3 Texas, in its Red River Rivalry matchup against Oklahoma, also won its game by a field goal, defeating the Sooners and remaining unbeaten.

No. 4 Virginia Tech lost to Georgia Tech 28-23. Maybe Virginia Tech just needs to stop playing games in Atlanta, where it's 0-2 this season.

No. 7 Ohio State lost to Purdue 26-18.

If Alabama is deemed the top team in the country by the polls this week or if it remains No. 2, it's just a number.

Winning makes the only case that matters and if Alabama keeps winning — even at No. 2 with SEC roommate Florida remaining at No. 1 — the two teams will meet in the national semifinal known as the SEC championship game, with the winner getting a shot at the national championship.

As one SEC philosopher has noted, it's all part of the process, and right now the process is working.

Alabama wide receiver Marquis Maze (4) and South Carolina cornerback C.C. Whitlock (12) battle for a first-quarter pass.

STAFF PHOTO/MARK ALMOND

ap top 10 released 10.18.09

TEAM	1ST	2ND	3RD	4TH	FINAL
ALABAMA	10	3	0	7	20
SOUTH CAROLINA	0	6	0	0	6

Attendance   92,012 Bryant Denny Stadium

SCORING SUMMARY

UA   M Barron 77 yd interception return (L Tiffin kick)
UA   L Tiffin 25 yd field goal, 7 plays, 31 yds, TOP 3:21
SC   S Lanning 22 yd field goal, 10 plays, 63 yds, TOP 2:38
UA   L Tiffin 35 yd field goal, 7 plays, 62 yds, TOP 2:18
SC   S Lanning 31 yd field goal, 8 plays, 45 yds, TOP 0:56
UA   M Ingram 4 yd run (L Tiffin kick), 6 plays, 68 yds, TOP 3:01

TEAM STATISTICS

	UA	SC
FIRST DOWNS	17	19
NET YARDS RUSHING	264	64
NET YARDS PASSING	92	214
COMPLETIONS-ATTEMPTS-INT	10-20-2	20-46-1
TOTAL OFFENSE YARDS	356	278
PENALTIES: NUMBER-YARDS	10-113	5-60
PUNTS-YARDS	3-136	7-308
PUNT RETURNS: NUMBER-YDS-TD	5-75-0	1-7-0
KICKOFF RETURNS: NUMBER-YDS-TD	2-45-0	5-111-0
POSSESSION TIME	28:17	31:43
SACKS BY: NUMBER-YARDS LOST	5-26	1-5
FIELD GOALS	2-3	2-3
FUMBLES: NUMBER-LOST	2-2	1-1

INDIVIDUAL OFFENSIVE STATISTICS

RUSHING: UA — M Ingram 24-246; R Upchurch 4-27; T Richardson 5-13;
            G McElroy 2-1
            SC — K Miles 15-40; S Garcia 9-19; M Brown 1-6
PASSING: UA — G McElroy 20-10-2, 92
            SC —S Garcia 46-20-1, 214
RECEIVING: UA — M Ingram 2-23; C Peek 2-21; M Maze 2-19; R Upchurch 2-18;
            T Richardson 2-11
            SC — J Barnes 6-46; A Jeffery 4-83; K Miles 4-28; W Saunders 3-38;
            P DiMarco 1-8; M Brown 1-8; D Moore 1-3

INDIVIDUAL DEFENSIVE STATISTICS

INTERCEPTIONS: UA — M Barron 1-77
                SC — S Wilson 1-15; C Whitlock 1-9
SACKS: UA —T King 1-1; E Anders 0-1, C Reamer 1-0, L Washington 1-0,
          B Deaderick 1-0
          SC — C Geathers 1-0
TACKLES: UA —M Barron 4-4; R McClain 5-2; T King 2-5; E Anders 1-6;
          C Reamer 3-3; J Woodall 4-1; L Washington 2-2
          SC — C Culliver 6-5; S Wilson 4-7; E Norwood 2-4; D Stewart 3-2;
          N Pepper 2-3; D Swearinger 2-1

1	2	3	4	5	6	7	8	9	10
ALABAMA	FLORIDA	TEXAS	USC	CINCINNATI	BOISE STATE	IOWA	MIAMI FLORIDA	LSU	TCU

Alabama running back Mark Ingram (22) breaks away from South Carolina free safety Chris Culliver (17) and South Carolina linebacker Josh Dickerson (41) in the second quarter.

STAFF PHOTO/MARK ALMOND

High-Water Mark

Ingram rushes for career-high 246 yards to lead No. 2 Tide over No. 22 South Carolina 20-6

By GENTRY ESTES

Tailback Mark Ingram was doing everything else for Alabama's offense on a chilly Saturday night.

Why not quarterback, too?

Three snaps for Ingram in the Wildcat and another into the end zone capped a late 68-yard drive to seal victory as the No. 2-ranked Crimson Tide survived its closest call this season.

An eventual 20-6 homecoming victory over No. 22 South Carolina was chalked up to another solid defensive effort and Ingram, who bailed out a struggling offense with a career night. Ingram had all six carries on the final scoring drive — including a 4-yard touchdown run with 4:54 to go — and finished with 246 yards on 24 carries, the third-best total in school history and the best ever in Bryant-Denny Stadium.

"The offense, we needed to make a play," Ingram said. "We needed to make something happen, and whenever they gave me the ball, I just tried to take advantage of my opportunity to make something happen."

The victory, while in doubt for much of the chilly evening, allowed Alabama to stay in the thick of the national race on a day when seemingly all the frontrunners stumbled but survived.

"I really think that's the sign of a good team," coach Nick Saban said after the Crimson Tide improved to 7-0, 4-0 in the SEC. "I'm proud of our players for being able to go out there and earn this and fight their way through it and do what they needed to do to win the game. You can say it's winning ugly or whatever, but it's still winning."

No. 1 Florida needed a last-minute field goal Saturday to edge Arkansas, while No. 3 Texas beat Oklahoma by three points.

After those dramatics, UA appeared set to roll through another weekend when former St. Paul's standout Mark Barron returned an interception 77 yards for a touchdown barely a minute into the game.

But it wouldn't be nearly so easy this time.

Four turnovers and an uncharacteristically poor performance by quarterback Greg McElroy slowed the offense and allowed the Gamecocks (5-2, 2-2) and coach Steve Spurrier to hang in a game they never led.

McElroy finished 10 of 20 for only 92 yards and two interceptions, including one on his first throw of the evening. No Alabama player caught more than two passes Saturday night, and Ingram — of course — led the team with 23 receiving yards.

"I'm going to have ups and downs. I knew that coming in," McElroy said. "You're going to have bad days. It's just one of those things. We got the win tonight, and I'm pleased with that."

As was the case against Ole Miss last weekend, Alabama's offense struggled in the red zone. Leigh Tiffin booted field goals of 25 and 35 yards before halftime and missed from 49 yards, leaving the score a perilous 13-6 at intermission.

It stayed there well into the fourth quarter. With Alabama's defense hanging on without cornerback Javier Arenas (rib injury) and still managing to thwart the Gamecocks each time, the Crimson Tide's offense took possession with 7:55 remaining and 68 yards to the end zone.

Ingram needed only six plays to travel all of it. He rolled 24 yards on the first snap, and then after another carry, he appeared after a timeout in the shotgun. Three Wildcat plays netted 36 yards, and Ingram crossed the final 4 yards on a toss to left, scoring the offense's first touchdown of the game with 4:54 to play.

"Mark did as a fine a job today as anybody I've ever been around," Saban said of Ingram. "That includes Ricky Williams and Ronnie Brown and some really good ones. He was fantastic."

South Carolina managed only 64 rushing yards on 27 carries, but Gamecocks quarterback Stephen Garcia threw for 214 yards on 20-of-46 passing. He scrambled to avoid recurring pressure and shrugged off five sacks to stay in the game.

"We did a few good things here and there but not enough to get into the game," Spurrier said. "Give credit to Alabama. They are a very good team, hard to learn against. Obviously, they ran it very well when they had the ball."

Saban said he was not surprised the game was close.

"I kind of had the feeling that this would be a tough game," Saban said. "Psychologically, this is a tough league to be at your best every week. Hopefully, our players learned a few things about what it takes on a consistent basis."

Tide's McElroy Promises to Figure Out His Slump

By JON SOLOMON

Alabama quarterback Greg McElroy didn't quite make a Tim Tebow promise Saturday night after a second straight rough outing.

A year ago after losing to Ole Miss, Tebow gave an impassioned speech, promising that no one would ever play as hard as he and his teammates the rest of the way. Florida won the national title.

There might not be a plaque put up on Alabama's campus from McElroy's comments, like Florida did with Tebow's. But the point was similar: The quarterback shouldered responsibility for No. 2 Alabama's ineffective passing game Saturday in a 20-6 victory over South Carolina.

"I haven't been playing real confidently. I haven't been stepping into my throws like I had been in weeks past," McElroy said. "But we'll get it figured out. I promise. I promised my fans and promised the coaches and promised to the players that I will get it figured out and we will get it straightened out.

"I don't care if I spend every second and sleep in the football complex. I will do that to figure this thing out. I have all the confidence in the world in myself and my teammates that we can come back and dominate opponents, just like we did against Arkansas and against other teams."

McElroy completed only 10 of 20 passes for 92 yards, tossed two interceptions and no touchdowns, and lost two fumbles.

In the past two games, he has been a 46 percent passer with no touchdowns and 119.5 passing yards per game and four turnovers. McElroy started the first five games of the season by completing 66 percent of his throws for 217.2 yards per game and nine touchdowns and one interception.

"The absence of explosive plays in the passing game and the inability for us to throw effectively in the last two games is something we definitely need to get corrected," Alabama coach Nick Saban said.

"We have to get our confidence back going in the passing game, and it's going to be something we need in the future."

Only two of McElroy's 10 completions Saturday went to wide receivers. Julio Jones was held without a catch for the first time in 20 career games. Marquis Maze could have had a long touchdown but he had to wait on McElroy's throw.

"When you're not throwing it very well, it's hard for your receivers to do what they can do, and we have too many good skill guys here not to utilize our skill guys on offense," Saban said.

McElroy also threw short on a screen pass to Roy Upchurch that could have been a touchdown. "It just slipped right out of my hands," McElroy said. "It was terrible. A JV high school quarterback could make that throw."

In each of the past two games, McElroy has spoken of not reading coverages well. "Obviously, this is my first time being in the woods, guys," McElroy said. "This is my first time in the SEC and I'm going to have some ups and downs, and I knew that coming in. This is new territory for me. I've never really struggled in the past."

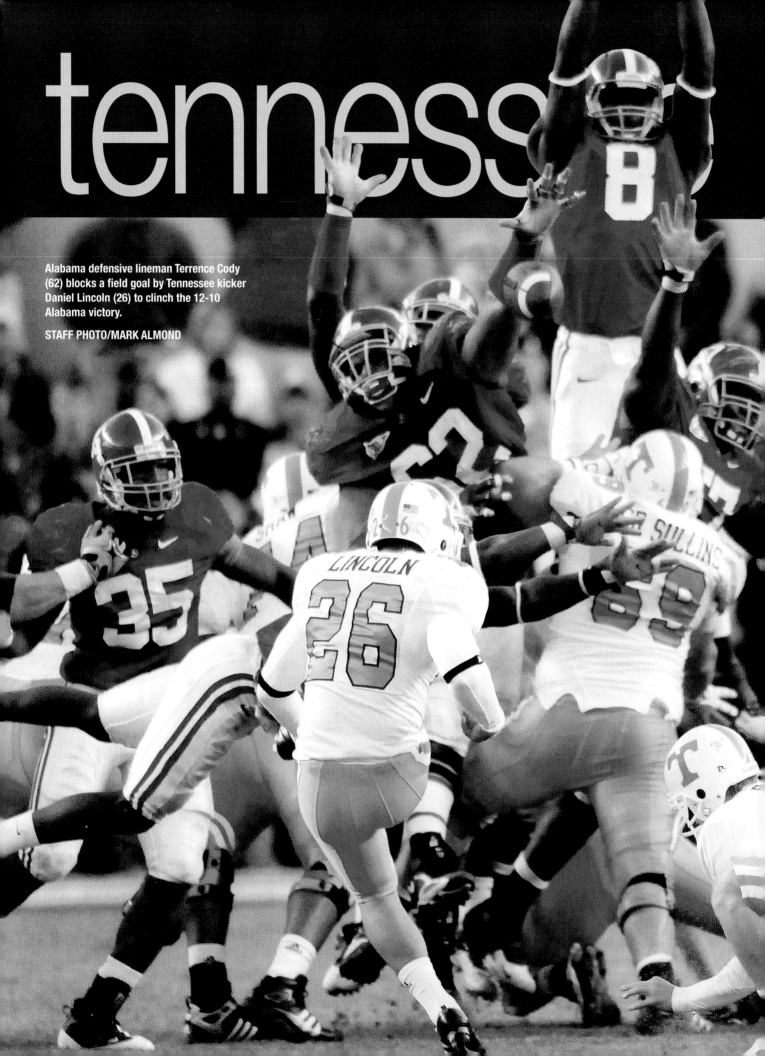

tenness

Alabama defensive lineman Terrence Cody (62) blocks a field goal by Tennessee kicker Daniel Lincoln (26) to clinch the 12-10 Alabama victory.

STAFF PHOTO/MARK ALMOND

CRIMSON TIDE | 12

VOLUNTEERS | 10

10.24.09 | 2:30 p.m. | Bryant-Denny Stadium | Tuscaloosa, AL

Good Ol' Rocky Block

"They'll be Talking About This Forever"

By RAY MELICK

If you doubted, you don't know your history. If you sat through the last 3:29, watching one apparent disaster after another befall Alabama and found yourself saying "Oh, no" over and over, then you don't know this football team.

"We never say, 'Oh, no,'" said Crimson Tide offensive tackle Drew Davis. "We're always thinking, 'Oh, yes.'"

Oh, yes, Alabama found a way to overcome the most disastrous three minutes of the season. In that three-minute stretch, Mark Ingram lost the first fumble of his Alabama career, the Alabama defense gave up its first touchdown in almost 12 quarters, Tennessee recovered an onsides kick that everyone knew was coming, and it drove deep enough into Alabama territory for the Vols' Daniel Lincoln to set up for what appeared to be a makeable, game-winning 44-yard field goal with just four seconds left.

But then the Tide's Terrence Cody planted his mammoth frame as firmly into the history of the Alabama-Tennessee rivalry as he planted Lincoln's field-goal attempt into the Bryant-Denny turf.

It wasn't pretty. For the first time this season the Tide was statistically dominated by an opponent, particularly in the second half.

This many things have never gone this wrong in such a short span for this team this season, and it began to get inside their heads.

But not the way you think.

"Yes, it got in my head," said cornerback Javier Arenas. "I began to say, 'It's time to make a play. It's time to make something happen. It's time to play Alabama football.'"

Alabama coach Nick Saban may have done away with many of the trappings of tradition -- the non-stop playing of "Rocky Top" all week, the scout team wearing Tennessee orange -- but that doesn't mean these players don't understand this rivalry.

"This is Tennessee," said linebacker Cory Reamer. "To beat Tennessee with a last-second block of a field goal -- this goes down in history. They'll be talking about this forever."

Maybe this outcome answers once and for all one of the questions that was asked of the legendary Paul "Bear" Bryant way back in 1966.

Alabama and Tennessee were involved in another game almost exactly like this one, with the Tide in the midst of what would be an undefeated season and hanging on to an 11-10 lead as Tennessee lined up for what seemed to be a last-second, game-winning field goal.

The kick was wide, prompting someone to ask Bryant what would have happened if the kick had been good.

"If he had kicked it straight," Bryant said, "we'd have blocked it."

No doubt. Not anymore.

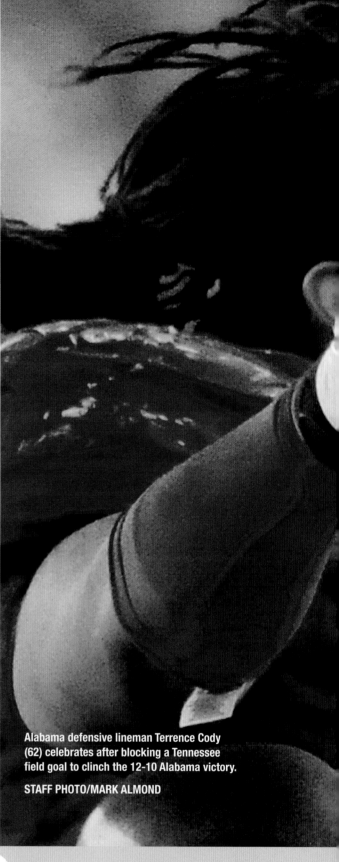

Alabama defensive lineman Terrence Cody (62) celebrates after blocking a Tennessee field goal to clinch the 12-10 Alabama victory.

STAFF PHOTO/MARK ALMOND

ap top 10 released 10.25.09

TEAM	1ST	2ND	3RD	4TH	FINAL
ALABAMA	3	6	0	3	12
TENNESSEE	0	3	0	7	10

Attendance   92,012 Bryant-Denny Stadium

SCORING SUMMARY

UA   L Tiffin 38 yd field goal, 10 plays, 49 yds, TOP 3:24
UT   D Lincoln 24 yd field goal, 11 plays, 63 yds, TOP 4:44
UA   L Tiffin 50 yd field goal, 8 plays, 22 yd, TOP 3:44
UA   L Tiffin 22 yd field goal, 13 plays, 64 yds, TOP 5:36
UA   L Tiffin 49 yd field goal, 7 plays, 31 yds, TOP 4:02
UT   G Jones 21 yd pass from J Crompton (D Lincoln kick), 8 plays, 43 yds, TOP 2:10

TEAM STATISTICS

	UA	UT
FIRST DOWNS	16	20
NET YARDS RUSHING	136	74
NET YARDS PASSING	120	265
COMPLETIONS-ATTEMPTS-INT	18-29-0	21-37-1
TOTAL OFFENSE YARDS	256	339
PENALTIES: NUMBER-YARDS	1-10	8-68
PUNTS-YARDS	3-132	5-185
PUNT RETURNS: NUMBER-YDS-TD	2-33-0	1-23-0
KICKOFF RETURNS: NUMBER-YDS-TD	1-30-0	5-142-0
POSSESSION TIME	27:42	32:18
SACKS BY: NUMBER-YARDS LOST	2-19	0-0
FIELD GOALS	4-4	1-4
FUMBLES: NUMBER-LOST	1-1	0-0

INDIVIDUAL OFFENSIVE STATISTICS

RUSHING: UA — M Ingram 18-99; G McElroy 3-22
            UT — M Hardesty 18-48; B Brown 11-35; M Teague 1-6, D Oku 1-2
PASSING: UA — G McElroy 29-18-0
            UT — J Cromton 36-21-1
RECEIVING: UA — J Jones 7-54; D Hanks 3-17; R Upchurch 2-6; M Maze 1-19;
            B Smelley 1-10; P Dial 1-4; B Huber 1-4; Michael Williams 1-4
            UT — G Jones 7-72, D Moore 4-73; M Hardesty 4-66; L Stocker 3-33;
            M Teague 2-17; A Johnson 1-4

INDIVIDUAL DEFENSIVE STATISTICS

INTERCEPTIONS: UA — M Barron 1-11
                UT — None
SACKS: UA — J Arenas 1-0; M Dareus 1-0   UT — 0
TACKLES: UA   J Arenas 8 6; M Barron 5 3; E Anders 2 6; N Johnson 2 6
                R McClain 1-7; C Reamer 2-5
                UT — R McCoy 6-6; S Frazier 1-6; D Rogan 5-1;
                D Williams 2-4; E Berry 2-3

1	2	3	4	5	6	7	8	9	10
FLORIDA	ALABAMA	TEXAS	USC	CINCINNATI	BOISE STATE	IOWA	TCU	LSU	OREGON

Perfection!   107

Not a Masterpiece, But a Beautiful Finish for Tide

By RANDY KENNEDY

Terrence Cody has never actually met Tennessee offensive lineman Cory Sullins.

But the mammoth Alabama nose tackle has spent enough time on the field with the 6-foot-1, 270-pound Volunteer to know what was going through the mind of the man lined up across from him on Saturday's final play.

"He was probably thinking 'Oh snap. Here we go again.'"

At some point, all eight of Alabama's opponents this season have had to face that emotion.

There are some undeniable weaknesses in the Alabama offense, and the Tide kick coverage teams provide an adventure every time they take the field, but somehow this Alabama team always finds a way to bring the opposition to that "here-we-go-again" moment.

The Tide has not dropped a regular-season game in 23 months (last losing at Auburn). During that span, some games have been blowouts and others have been decided in the fourth quarter. But none has produced a finish as dramatic as Saturday's 12-10 win over bitter rival Tennessee.

Cody's blocked field goal with no time showing on the clock produced an explosion from the crowd that may have been louder than any ever heard at Bryant-Denny Stadium.

"It was real emotional and thrilling," said Cody, the 6-5, 354-pound (give or take a dreadlock or two) fan favorite. "I knew it was crunch time. Once I knocked him (Sullins) on his back, I just closed my eyes and reached up with my left hand."

The block was Cody's second of the game. But if not for fans wanting to hang around to sing Rammer Jammer, many of the 92,012 would have probably missed it.

With four minutes remaining, Alabama was in complete control. Leading 12-3 — which amounted to three scores ahead in a game that had not produced a single touchdown — Alabama had the ball and a first down on its 38. With a running back who has never lost a fumble in his entire career, it seemed clear that a couple of handoffs to Mark Ingram would close out the game.

But Ingram lost a fumble with 3:29 remaining when Eric Berry stripped the ball and then recovered it. Ingram may still win the Heisman, but Berry was the best player on that play and the best player on the field all day Saturday.

Still, Alabama found a way to survive despite playing poorly at times and facing a Tennessee team that has started to come to life under first-year coach Lane Kiffin.

Some enterprising artist may make a painting of Saturday's final heroics (just in time for Christmas gift season), but the Tide's overall performance Saturday was anything but a work of art.

In the last three weeks, Alabama's offense has scored a total of two touchdowns. Safety Mark Barron (with one touchdown) is the Tide's third-leading scorer over the last two games behind kicker Leigh Tiffin and Ingram.

In October, Alabama has scored, in order, 38, 22, 20 and 12 points. That's a disturbing trend for a team with national championship aspirations.

But all the Tide's season goals are still intact thanks to Cody's last-second dramatics.

(15) Darius Hanks misses pass as Tennessee (14) DB Eric Berry puts on the pressure in 1st half.

STAFF PHOTO/GLENN BAESKE

Tiffin's Toe Delivers Alabama

By DOUG SEGREST

There's no place like home for Leigh Tiffin. That's because he doesn't like it there.

"Of all the stadiums we've played in, this is my least favorite," Tiffin said about Bryant-Denny Stadium after top-ranked Alabama's 12-10 victory against archrival Tennessee on Saturday afternoon. "It's always swirling. You can't tell which way the wind is blowing."

Regardless, the record-setting Alabama kicker survived the elements and added to his reputation when he accounted for Alabama's lone points in the win with four field goals despite the wind.

One field goal went 50 yards, the longest of the season for the senior legacy. Another was just a few inches shy of covering half the distance of a football field.

Don't think he speaks the truth? Just ask Tennessee's Daniel Lincoln.

Tiffin's counterpart missed three field goals on the day -- two courtesy of the paws of Terrence Cody, who blocked both of Lincoln's fourth-quarter efforts, including the game-winning attempt as time expired.

Another one, at the end of the first half, died in a jet stream just shy of the goalpost after a 46-yard flight.

But Tiffin was true every time.

"He negotiated both of those (long ones)," Tide coach Nick Saban said. "It was the difference in the game."

Give Steve Spurrier at least some of the credit. Following Alabama's 20-6 victory last week, when Tiffin outscored the Gamecocks 8-6 on his own, Spurrier accused the kicker of using tape to mark his kicks - an NCAA no-no to which few teams and officials pay heed.

"I need to thank Coach Spurrier for getting my focus and concentration level back," Tiffin deadpanned. "So much attention was paid to what was really a non-story.

"Sometimes we use tape, grass -- whatever we find (to mark the ball). It's only used to help me line up. It doesn't make one bit of difference."

So what did Tiffin use against Tennessee? A finger, marking the spot until holder P.J. Fitzgerald settled into position.

Leigh Tiffin the senior has come a long way from the nervous freshman who missed three field goals in an overtime loss at Arkansas in 2006.

Tiffin admits he's a different kicker now, thanks to maturity and confidence.

And it took confidence, especially on his final kick of the day -- a 49-yarder with 4:02 left in the game that seemed to put the contest out of reach.

By then, the wind had picked up and the pressure had intensified. And, as he did on his 50-yarder in the first half, Tiffin just lifted a line drive that barely got above the post.

"They weren't strong kicks. But I felt they were good. I didn't get a lot of loft."

Before the game, as he does before every one, Tiffin told Saban what he thought his maximum range would be. In ideal situations, he said, it's 60 yards. Saturday, it was 52.

Consider this: Of the 21 field goals of 50 yards or more kicked in Alabama history, Van and Leigh Tiffin are responsible for 11.

But one thing Van, an All American in the 1980s has over his son, is a time-expiring kick to beat Auburn in the 1985 Iron Bowl.

Leigh Tiffin has had his moments. But he still wants one like Pop.

"Everyone wants that moment," he said. "You think it would be nerve-wracking, but it's when you're most relaxed. I'd like to get one before I leave."

(99) Leigh Tiffin kicks for 3 of his points in 1st half. Holding is (7) P. J. Fitzgerald.
STAFF PHOTO/GLENN BAESKE

lsu

CRIMSON TIDE | 24
TIGERS | 15

| Tuscaloosa, AL

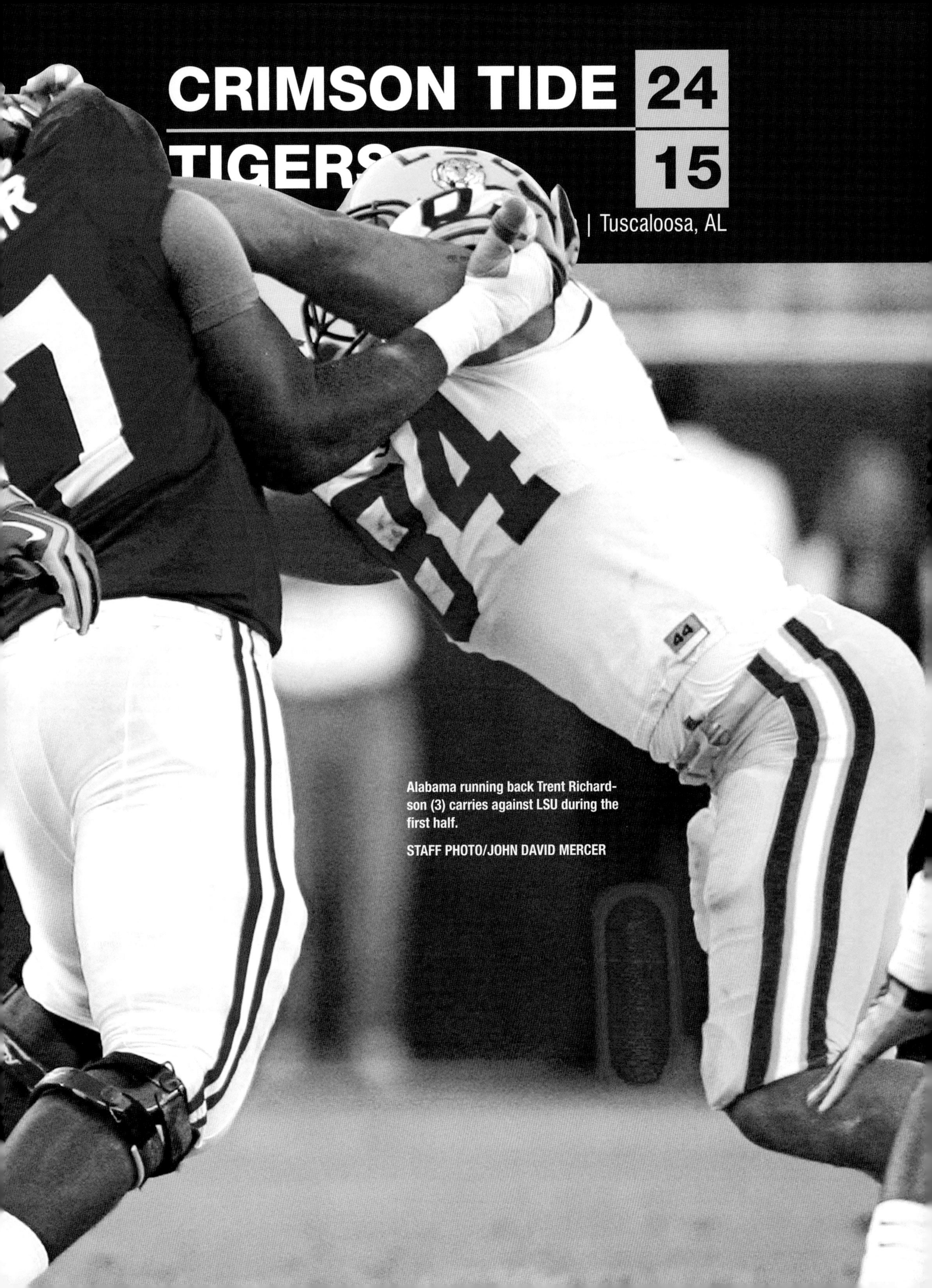

Alabama running back Trent Richardson (3) carries against LSU during the first half.

STAFF PHOTO/JOHN DAVID MERCER

"Highway 8" Julio

By MARK McCARTER

It's a few minutes after the game and the last "we just beat the hell out of you" echoes through the stands. There is noise and chaos and relief and jubilation and amazement as dusk settles about us in the aftermath of Alabama's 24-15 win over LSU.

Let's walk along this sideline in front of the Alabama bench, headed toward the north end zone. We're not walking on a mere field now. We're walking on a path of history. It's just grass and dirt, but soon enough, they may repave it with gold. Almost certainly, Alabama will officially rename this stretch of football field Highway 8.

It was this direct route that Julio Jones -- No. 1 in the recruiting charts, No. 8 in your program and pretty much No. 0 when it came to recent involvement in Alabama's offense -- followed to a touchdown.

It was a 73-yard trip to the SEC West title. It showed, Mapquest notwithstanding, that it was 73 yards from Tuscaloosa to Atlanta, site of the SEC Championship game. And, just maybe, 73 yards to merge with yet another road, toward a national championship.

"That's why we play, to win championships," quarterback Greg McElroy said.

It didn't come easily or without drama and controversy.

There was an LSU interception with 5:54 to play that wasn't ... but maybe was.

That came on the opposite sideline from Highway 8. Turned out to be a dead end for LSU. Patrick Peterson picked off a McElroy pass in front of the Tigers' bench.

"An 'oh, shoot,' moment," McElroy said.

A considerable number of LSU fans likely opted for stronger language when official Gerald Hodges determined that it was not a theft.

By that point, LSU was being held together by duct tape anyway. Backups were in at quarterback and tailback. You're not sure LSU had enough to have capitalized anyway. We'll never know.

What you do know is that Alabama quite nicely capitalized on a fresh - and refreshed - offensive outlook. It opened with seven consecutive passes. It was, said coach Nick Saban, "a different way to play our hand."

Offensive coordinator Jim McIlwain opted for more balance -- 34 passes, 38 runs -- to give tailback Mark Ingram less LSU attention and more opportunity. He didn't clinch the Heisman with his 144 yards but it won't hurt the campaign.

Meanwhile, there was Jones. He's been a Ferrari parked in the garage and nobody could seem to even find the keys. But 4 1/2 minutes into the fourth quarter, Jones eased his way to the left sideline, hauled in a soap bubble of a pass from McElroy, got past one turnstile of tacklers and went Usain Bolt down the field.

Marveled McElroy, "I've never seen somebody run so fast in my life."

"The whole game we were bending a little bit," LSU's Kelvin Sheppard said, "but we never broke until that play."

Jones, who spends his words as if working with a quota, said "I needed to make a play and I did."

People have been saying that for weeks.

As you knew he would, artist Daniel Moore, who has magnificently captured Alabama football history on canvas for decades, quickly began work on a painting of Terrence Cody's game-saving block of the Tennessee field goal.

Note to Daniel: You might want to set up two easels in your studio. Highway 8 is just waiting to be painted.

ap top 10 released 11.01.09

Alabama linebacker Jerrell Harris (10) and Alabama defensive back Chris Rogers (1) smother LSU safety Ron Brooks (13) on the opening kickoff.

STAFF PHOTO/MARK ALMOND

TEAM	1ST	2ND	3RD	4TH	FINAL
ALABAMA	0	3	7	14	24
LSU	0	7	8	0	15

Attendance   92,012 Bryant-Denny Stadium

SCORING SUMMARY

LSU   D Peterson 12 yd pass from J Jefferson(J Jasper kick), 13 plays, 91 yds, TOP 6:11
UA   L Tiffin 28 yd field goal, 8 plays, 40 yds, TOP 3:20
LSU   Team saftey
LSU   S Ridley 8 yd run (J Lee pass failed), 6 plays, 59 yds, TOP 2:36
UA   L Tiffin 20 yd field goal, 12 plays, 65 yds, TOP 5:44
UA   J Jones 73 pass from G McElroy, 1 play, 73 yds, TOP 0:13
UA   L Tiffin 40 yd field goal, 11 plays, 31 yards, TOP 6:14

TEAM STATISTICS

	UA	LSU
FIRST DOWNS	24	13
NET YARDS RUSHING	176	95
NET YARDS PASSING	276	158
COMPLETIONS-ATTEMPTS-INT	19-34-1	14-27-1
TOTAL OFFENSE YARDS	452	253
PENALTIES: NUMBER-YARDS	4-20	8-43
PUNTS-YARDS	4-151	8-373
PUNT RETURNS: NUMBER-YDS-TD	4-11-0	0-0-0
KICKOFF RETURNS: NUMBER-YDS-TD	3-78-0	5-106-0
POSSESSION TIME	32:52	27:08
SACKS BY: NUMBER-YARDS LOST	3-27	1-2
FIELD GOALS	3-3	0-0
FUMBLES: NUMBER-LOST	1-0	0-0

INDIVIDUAL OFFENSIVE STATISTICS

RUSHING: UA – M Ingram 22-144; T Richardson 6-27; G McElroy 6-21
                    LSU– C Scott 13-83; J Jefferson 7-16; S Ridley 2-8; T Holliday 1-2
PASSING: UA – G McElroy 19-34-1, 276
                    LSU – J Jefferson 10-17-0, 114; J Lee 4-10-1, 44
RECEIVING: UA – M Maze 6-88; M Ingram 5-30; J Jones 4-102; M Williams 2-25;
                    D Hanks 1-21; B Smelley 1-10
                    LSU – T Toliver 4-46; B Lafell 4-28; D Peterson 2-40; R.J. Jackson 2-26
                    R Shepard 2-18

INDIVIDUAL DEFENSIVE STATISTICS

INTERCEPTIONS: UA – R Green 1-0
                    LSU – K Sheppard 1-1
SACKS: UA –M Dareus 2-0; N Johnson 1-0   LS – D Nevis 1-0
TACKLES: UA – R McClain 1-8; J Arenas 4-3; M Barron 3-4; C Reamer 1-4;
                    M Johnson 3-1; M Dareus 2-2; E Anders 2-2; K Jackson 1-3
                    LSU – J Cutrera 4-7; P Riley 4-4; K Sheppard 4-4; D Nevis 2-5;
                    J Eugene 6-0; C Hawkins 2-2; L Edwards 1-3; C Jones 1-3

1	2	3	4	5	6	7	8	9	10
FLORIDA	TEXAS	ALABAMA	CINCINNATI	BOISE STATE	TCU	OREGON	IOWA	LSU	GEORGIA TECH

LSU can't keep up with Bama's Jones

Wide receiver responds to taunting with big play as Tide wraps up SEC West crown

By GENTRY ESTES

Last week's verbal jabs from LSU cornerback Patrick Peterson toward Alabama receiver Julio Jones were nothing compared to ones in person.

It got to a point where Jones, the coolest customer you'll find despite being a popular target for speculative criticism during his sophomore season, had heard enough.

"I guess he got real flustered, and he said, 'They say I'm not great. Well, we're going to show them right now,'" Crimson Tide quarterback Greg McElroy said. "He sure did."

With Alabama's season hanging in the balance, wouldn't Jones have to be the one to keep it rolling along? Saturday's pivotal 24-15 victory over LSU turned on a short fourth-quarter screen pass. The former Foley High star snagged it, turned up the sideline and simply outran everybody for a 73-yard touchdown.

"I didn't look back," Jones said.

The score gave the Crimson Tide the lead for good with 10:24 remaining in the game and continued a dramatic turnaround for a slumping offense that regained its stride against a fearsome LSU defense that didn't have enough in the end.

Jones' play, two field goals and a two-point conversion allowed the third-ranked Crimson Tide to outscore the ninth-ranked Tigers 14-0 in the fourth quarter and clinched the program's second consecutive SEC Western Division title before a

delirious crowd of 92,012 at Bryant-Denny Stadium.

Alabama (9-0, 6-0 SEC) now is assured of a Dec. 5 reunion with top-ranked Florida in the SEC championship game. The Gators, of course, beat the Crimson Tide last season en route to their national title.

For the second season in a row, the Crimson Tide clinched its date in Atlanta by surviving a gritty, physical slugfest with LSU (7-2, 4-2). Nick Saban's squad represented the last ones standing in a contest with brutal licks and plentiful injuries.

It was a contest after Saban's heart.

"I'm extremely pleased and happy that we won the West," Saban said, "and we now control our own destiny in terms of what else we can accomplish. It was a tough, physical game and, man, those games are fun to be a part of."

"Our football team played awfully

It Starts With the Mountain in the Middle

By DON KAUSLER JR.

It starts with the mountain in the middle. There's a moat in front of the goal line, a brick wall at the line of scrimmage and barbed-wire fences in the secondary.

This is the fortress Alabama's defense has built inside Bryant-Denny Stadium, and veterans guard it like a red army. Gen. Rolando McClain and his troops have all but posted "No Trespassing" signs outside and "Keep Out" signs at the 20-yard line.

A unit that has allowed only three rushing touchdowns this season has allowed only one since its opener, and this inhospitable host has not allowed any in five home games.

Opponents trying to climb over or around Mount Cody -- Terrence Cody, the Tide's 354-pound senior nose guard -- are averaging only 2.2 yards per rush, but that average is 1.9 yards at home.

The secret?

"We've all bought into the program," said McClain, the third-ranked Crimson Tide's star junior middle linebacker. "Besides the hard work, it's like we are a band of brothers out there."

The Tide is averaging more than two interceptions for every touchdown pass it has allowed. Opponents have a third-down conversion rate of only .298.

Their touchdown rate in the red zone is only .357.

Accountability is a key.

"We don't want to let the guy beside us down," McClain said of a quality instilled by coach Nick Saban. "That's the important thing, and that's what he has put in us. . . .

"We give our all on every play, so we don't let him down. You don't want to be that guy that messes up a play, because everybody has to be accountable for what they do on the field, and accountability is what he's taught us."

As No. 9 LSU gets set to step into this hostile environment for a 2:30 p.m. showdown Saturday, it's a good time to measure the progress of a defense that has Alabama (8-0, 5-0) on the verge of a second consecutive Western Division championship.

Two years ago, Alabama allowed five touchdowns and 475 yards in a 41-34 loss to an LSU team that went on to win the national championship. Five current starters either started or played extensively in that game.

Last year, Alabama allowed three touchdowns and 382 yards in a 27-21 overtime victory at LSU. Three more players who will start Saturday started in that game.

This Alabama defense had eight returning starters, and that didn't count defensive end Lorenzo Washington, the starting nose guard two years ago.

"Our success this year comes from our guys playing with each other for three years," McClain said. "We're a lot more comfortable with each other.

Alabama defensive lineman Terrence Cody (62) celebrates.

STAFF PHOTO/MARK ALMOND

Alabama wide receiver Julio Jones (8) leaves LSU defenders in his wake as he runs 73 yards for a touchdown in the fourth quarter.

STAFF PHOTO/MARK ALMOND

. . . Being comfortable allows us to play faster, and that's where our success comes from."

Senior linebacker Cory Reamer says experience means many things become second nature.

"Now they can add stuff," he said of the coaches. "Now they can change the way we do stuff. Make calls. Run blitzes. Which makes it an even more dynamic defense."

LSU will bring its own rugged defense to town. The Tigers are ranked seventh in the nation in scoring defense (12.1 points per game), but Alabama ranks fifth (11.4). The Tigers are ranked 15th in the nation in total defense (293 yards per game), but the Tide is ranked fourth (240.6).

But if you're looking for a key statistic that separates the two teams, it's this: Alabama is tied for the SEC lead with 23 sacks. LSU ranks last with 11. And Alabama leads the SEC in fewest sacks allowed (eight). LSU ranks 11th (23).

All week, Alabama's key offensive starters have raved about the defense they will face. But backup running back Roy Upchurch paused when asked if this will be the toughest defense the Tide has faced this season.

"Mmmm . . . not the toughest," he said. "The toughest I've seen is our defense."

well," Tigers coach Les Miles said. "They played hard at times. Congratulations to Alabama. They're a fine football team. They played extremely well. I understand what happened. I'm just unhappy with the outcome."

LSU led 7-3 at halftime and used a safety to spur a touchdown drive to seize a 15-10 lead entering the fourth quarter. But Alabama owned the final moments of a bout ultimately decided by way of technical knockout. The Tigers were beat up physically, suffering a string of injuries to key personnel that made a difference in the decisive final minutes.

Topping the list was Peterson, who limped off multiple times because of cramps. Starting quarterback Jordan Jefferson (ankle) and starting tailback Charles Scott (collarbone) were not able to finish after fast starts.

Backup quarterback Jarrett Lee threw the final 10 passes as LSU's lead slipped away in the fourth quarter. An interception by Robby

Green, a New Orleans native, finished off the Tigers' final opportunity.

"To watch your team try as hard as they can to put points on the board, and I'm not able to help them," Jefferson said, "it is just devastating having to watch that from the sidelines."

Saban spent the bye week assuring fans that Alabama would come out with "guns a-blazing," and then lived up to it. McElroy threw on the first seven snaps and wound up firing 25 times before halftime.

The ploy spread out LSU's defense and helped Ingram gain 106 of his game-high 144 rushing yards in the second half.

"It was the way we planned the game," Saban said. "It was a little different way to play our hand, but I thought it worked effectively and, hopefully, surprised them a little bit at the beginning. As the game went on, we got more and more control of the line of scrimmage and more control of the game."

"We both wanted it real

bad," Ingram said. "We both played with a lot of passion and intensity. We were both standing in the way of a particular goal a team has, so it's going to be a physical game."

McElroy finished 19-of-34 passing for 276 yards — his second-best total of the season — and two touchdowns. Receiver Marquis Maze caught a career-high six passes for 88 yards in the first half, while Jones finished with 102 yards on four catches.

McElroy said he and Jones answered criticism that built during a stretch where the offense managed only two touchdowns in 14 quarters.

"He's had a lot of pressure on him, too," McElroy said of Jones. "I've had to deal with a lot of animosity and a lot of hatred from a lot of different people, which some of it was undeserved, I feel like. But sometimes, you've got to do what you've got to do. (Jones) has dealt with the same thing, and the fact he was able to make a play really made me excited for him and the team."

miss. state

CRIMSON TIDE | 31
BULLDOGS | 3

11.14.09 | 6:00 p.m. | Davis Wade Stadium | Starkville, MS

Alabama running back Mark Ingram (22) runs for a 70-yard touchdown in the fourth quarter.

STAFF PHOTO/MARK ALMOND

Listen Here!

Tide rings up another win

By MARK McCARTER

Hello ... hello ... hello ...

Will somebody answer that, please?

Sorry. There is a ringing in my ears that I don't figure will end until Wednesday.

Greg Byrne, the athletic director at Mississippi State, promised a great environment. The record-setting crowd and university delivered. Especially with their constant, merry, defiant ringing of cowbells.

Which made it a great environment here Saturday in Alabama's 31-3 win over the Bulldogs.

Assuming you didn't, you know, like, need to hear yourself think.

Or play football.

Only school bus drivers, jackhammer operators and the producers of "The View" have to work under such trying conditions of loud, incessant noise as do visiting teams at Davis Wade Stadium.

Warning: Obscure pop culture reference ahead:

"All I kept thinking about all week," said Tide quarterback Greg McElroy, "was the Will Ferrell ("Saturday Night Live") skit, 'More Cowbell.' I watched that a couple of times this week to get ready. Not really."

"I got a fever," actor Christopher Walken says in the skit, which is about a rock band. "And the only prescription is more cowbell."

That seems to be the prescription here, too.

Not only do Mississippi State fans have the same sort of obedience to the SEC rule against artificial noisemakers that as Al Capone did for Prohibition, they seem to have brought even more cowbells than usual.

It will be really terrific for them, and really scary for the rest of the free world, when first-year coach Dan Mullen can assemble enough athletes in Starkville to match his philosophy and the enthusiasm.

"They've done a good job over here," Alabama coach Nick Saban said. "They've got a difficult scheme to defend."

"They have the right man for the job here," McElroy said.

Mullen tried a psychological ploy of switching to black jerseys between warm-ups and kickoff, and the Bulldogs were frenetic as first-graders on Red Bull before the game.

"We expected it a little bit," Saban said. "I could tell by the way their players were in pregame it was going to be a street fight out there and we'd have to change the way we think and the way we play and the way we execute."

Now, to the undying credit of Alabama's football players, they seemed to have cotton balls stuffed in their ears. They were undaunted.

They played the quintessential Alabama game. This is a team, to use a boxing analogy, that may not pummel an opponent to an early TKO. But look up at the end, it's won every round decisively. Alabama played with surgical focus, consistently superb execution and big plays when it needed them.

Two Marquis Johnson breakups of touchdown passes. A Greg McElroy drive-rescuing scramble. A Mark Ingram burst. A 48-yard McElroy bomb to a wide-open Julio Jones. ("I didn't know Greg could throw it that far," teased offensive lineman Drew Davis.) A gotcha! call from offensive coordinator Jim McElwain, just when it seemed blase and predictable.

The sort of stuff that wins championships.

"Like I told our team, I think our best football is still out there some place," Saban said. "We need to focus on improving."

There was a scary moment when it seemed Alabama might be on the verge of becoming an ordinary football team instead of a championship one.

Ingram, the Tide's most valuable asset, scored on a one-yard plunge behind the blocking of Terrence Cody, often employed on short yardage to mimic a bulldozer going through a pine thicket.

Ingram didn't get up from the ground for several moments.

When he finally jogged to the bench, Alabama's training staff was all over him like a NASCAR pit stop. They even came up with duct tape to repair a dent. OK, it was really a bandage next to his right eye.

Now, anything for the rest of us to bandage our ears?

Alabama defensive back Marquis Johnson (24) breaks up a pass meant for Mississippi State wide receiver Brandon McRae (6).

STAFF PHOTO/ MARK ALMOND

ap top 10 released 11.15.09

TEAM	1ST	2ND	3RD	4TH	FINAL
ALABAMA	0	14	3	14	31
MISSISSIPPI STATE	0	0	0	3	3

Attendance   58,103 Davis Wade Stadium

SCORING SUMMARY

UA   D Hanks 45 yd pass from G McElroy (L Tiffin kick), 6 plays, 80 yds, TOP 3:04
UA   M Ingram 1 yd run (L Tiffin kick), 11 plays, 72 yds, TOP 6:14
UA   L Tiffin 39 yd field goal, 7 plays, 47 yd, TOP 3:32
MS   D DePasquale 34 yd field goal, 15 plays, 44 yds, TOP 6:59
UA   J Jones 48 pass from G McElroy (L Tiffin kick), 1 play, 48 yds, TOP 0:08
UA   M Ingram 70 yd run (L Tiffin kick), 1 play, 70 yds, TOP 0:11

TEAM STATISTICS

TEAM STATISTICS	UA	MS
FIRST DOWNS	17	11
NET YARDS RUSHING	252	114
NET YARDS PASSING	192	99
COMPLETIONS-ATTEMPTS-INT	13-18-0	9-20-3
TOTAL OFFENSE YARDS	444	213
PENALTIES: NUMBER-YARDS	3-25	2-14
PUNTS-YARDS	5-206	5-198
PUNT RETURNS: NUMBER-YDS-TD	1-0-0	1-2-0
KICKOFF RETURNS: NUMBER-YDS-TD	2-70-0	6-212-0
POSSESSION TIME	31:36	28:24
SACKS BY: NUMBER-YARDS LOST	2-18	0-0
FIELD GOALS	1-1	1-2
FUMBLES: NUMBER-LOST	0-0	1-0

INDIVIDUAL OFFENSIVE STATISTICS

RUSHING: UA — M Ingram 19-149; T Richardson 11-47; G McElroy 4-30;
            R Upchurch 5-19; M Maze 1-7
            MS — A Dixon 22-81; R Elliott 1-26; C Relf 6-19; B Heavens 1-5
PASSING: UA — G McElroy 18-13-0, 192
            MS — T Lee 17-9-2, 99; C Relf 3-0-1, 0
RECEIVING: UA — J Jones 4-66; M Maze 4-55; D Hanks 3-59; M Ingram 1-9;
            R Upchurch 1-3
            MS — A Dixon 6-59; C Bumphis 2-28; O Wilder 1-12

INDIVIDUAL DEFENSIVE STATISTICS

INTERCEPTIONS: UA — M Barron 2-0; M Johnson 1-0
                MS — None
SACKS: UA — C Reamer 1-0; R McClain 1-0   MS — None
TACKLES: UA — R McClain 9-2; C Reamer 5-2; J Woodall 4-2; K Jackson 4-2;
            M Barron 3-2; E Anders 2-2
            MS — C White 4-4; J Chaney 3-5; K Love 3-4; J Banks 3-4;
            C Mitchell 4-2; P McPhee 3-3

1	2	3	4	5	6	7	8	9	10
FLORIDA	ALABAMA	TEXAS	TCU	CINCINNATI	BOISE STATE	GEORGIA TECH	PITTSBURGH	OHIO STATE	LSU

Perfection! 119

When Will SEC Foes Learn? Can't Black Out Bama

By KEVIN SCARBINSKY

You can change your shirts, change your colors, change your stripes.

You can hang up a big, honking, high-def TV and crank up the volume till your guests' ears bleed.

You can invite everyone you know to the party, turn your head if they bring cowbells and play dumb when they ring them till the cows come home.

Almost anything is possible if you're a football program in the Southeastern Con-ference and Alabama's coming to town.

Anything but this.

You can't beat Alabama with cowbells and whistles.

When you have to bang your head against solid, physical, fundamental football for 60 long, hard minutes, almost anything else rings hollow.

Mississippi State warmed up in its traditional maroon jerseys Saturday, retreated to the locker room and came out -- for the first time in school history - in black shirts.

Mississippi State packed more people than ever into Davis Wade Stadium, and from the sound of things, every one of the 58,103 partygoers brought a cowbell or two.

Mississippi State tried every trick in the book.

The moral of the story: Alabama 31, Mississippi State 3.

Nick Saban must've been amused when another set of Bulldogs, following in the foolish footsteps of Georgia 2008, made a wardrobe change look like a wardrobe malfunction.

Right, coach?

"Um, I didn't really even sort of know that they didn't have their regular stuff on," Saban said. "I worry about our team. I don't really worry about the other team that much. Everybody's gotta do what they do.

"I'm an old traditionalist."

Yeah. He believes in old-school things. Like blocking and tackling.

One block in this game, when it was a scoreless game, made the point.

The key blow wasn't delivered by a lineman or tight end. It came instead from an unusual place.

Trent Richardson is a five-star true freshman running back. Members of that special breed sometimes don't see the field as much as they might because they can't, won't or don't do the little things without the ball in their hands.

Like block.

Richardson was the lone back on Alabama's first drive of the second quarter. He was the last man standing between a Mississippi State defensive back coming fast and free off the edge and a dangerous lick on quarterback Greg McElroy.

Actually, Richardson wasn't standing between the blitzer and the quarterback. He had to move across McElroy in a hurry to get to the blitzer before the blitzer got to the quarterback.

Richardson did his job, made the block

Alabama linebacker Rolando McClain (25) sacks Mississippi State quarterback Chris Relf (14). STAFF PHOTO/ MARK ALMOND

and gave McElroy time.

McElroy did his job, hitting a wide-open Darius Hanks for a 45-yard touchdown.

"Trent did a really good job on that one," Saban said. "That's the only way we could throw the ball."

It was solid, physical, fundamental football, and it came dressed in a simple white shirt and pants complete with a simple red hat.

Saban may not have noticed or cared that State changed its colors, but his players did. They flashed back a year to Georgia's misguided blackout.

"Last time somebody came out in black the same thing happened," senior linebacker Cory Reamer said. "We take it as an insult. We came out and gave it to (the State players). They were talking before the game and dancing all over the field."

Talking and dancing and making fashion statements all have their place in this world. That place is not on a football field.

Not with Alabama on the other side of the line.

No Letdown as Tide Takes Care of Business

By DON KAUSLER JR.

Dominant defense? Check.
Red-zone touchdown? Check.
Explosive plays? Check, check, check.

Third-ranked Alabama took care of business Saturday night, taking a 14-0 halftime lead and pulling away for a 31-3 victory over Mississippi State.

So much for a letdown.

The defense did a little bending, but it forced four consecutive three-and-outs to close the first half, it didn't allow a touchdown and sophomore strong safety Mark Barron intercepted two passes.

The offense wasn't quite a well-oiled machine, but three big plays – two touchdown passes by Greg McElroy and a long run by Mark Ingram – were more than enough to give the Tide its first comfortable victory in more than a month.

Not a bad way to bounce back from a draining 24-15 victory over LSU that earned the Crimson Tide the Southeastern Conference Western Division championship last week.

The best news for the Tide: Ingram

Alabama defensive backs Robby Green (23) and Marquis Johnson (24) celebrate Johnson's interception of a Mississippi State pass.
STAFF PHOTO/MARK ALMOND

was not seriously injured after his 2-yard touchdown run late in the second quarter. He sat out the last two series of the half with a cut over his right eye, but he carried on the first snap of the second half and went on to put the game away with a 70-yard touchdown run in the fourth quarter.

"I think the word to describe it is professional," Alabama senior cornerback Javier Arenas said.

"We're not a kid ... and getting complacent and not playing your best when you're up and playing down to the level of your opponents.

"We came out here to handle business. Coach (Nick) Saban kept drilling it in us, and we adopted that tendency and came out here and carried on."

It was the first easy victory for the third-ranked Crimson Tide (10-0, 7-0 in the Southeastern Confer-

ence) in a month. Alabama was coming off the emotional victory that earned it a rematch with No. 1 Florida in the SEC Championship Game.

At the end of a scoreless first quarter, this game had the makings of another close one.

"I told our players it was going to be a street fight out there," Saban said.

McElroy threw a 40-yard touchdown pass to Darius Hanks in the first half and a 48-yard touchdown pass to Julio Jones in the fourth quarter.

Mississippi State missed a field-goal attempt in the third quarter but made one in the fourth quarter to cut its deficit to 17-3.

That's when the Tide shifted its offense into another gear.

On the first play from scrimmage, McElroy threw to Jones, who was wide open in the middle of the field, for a score.

On the first play from scrimmage on the Tide's next possession, Ingram broke through a big hole in the middle and outraced the Bulldogs' defensive backs to the goal line 70 yards down the field.

Ingram's 2-yard touchdown run in the second quarter ended some red-zone futility for the Tide. It had scored only one touchdown in its past 12 trips inside an opponent's 20-yard line, a stretch that covered four games.

Mississippi State reached the red zone three times but came away with only three points. It missed a field goal on one possession in the third quarter that came after a kickoff return for an apparent touchdown was brought back to the 38-yard line, where Chad Bumpis stepped out of bounds.

Midway through the fourth quarter, after Ingram's long touchdown run, the Bulldogs drove to Alabama's 17-yard line, but a sack by linebacker Rolando McClain killed the threat.

Marquis Johnson intercepted a pass late in the game for the Tide. He also broke up two long passes at the goal line in the third quarter.

"I think our best football is still out there someplace," Saban said. "We really have to focus as a team and continue to get better."

tenn. ch

CRIMSON TIDE 45

OCS 0

nny Stadium | Tuscaloosa, AL

Alabama wide receiver Darius Hanks (15) leads Alabama running back Mark Ingram (22) to the goaline for a second-quarter touchdown.

STAFF PHOTO/ MARK ALMOND

Bama Gives Mocs the Boot

Ingram rushes for 102 yards and two TDs in 45-0 rout

By GENTRY ESTES

Once Alabama's Mark Ingram weaved 40 yards for his second touchdown in about 20 minutes of one-sided football, coach Nick Saban stopped him as he jogged to the sideline.

"I was pretty much done unless I had to go back in," Ingram said.

Alabama's starters took care of business early Saturday, allowing the bench to clear in their place. Young reserves and seldom-used seniors polished off an expectedly easy 45-0 victory over Tennessee-Chattanooga that involved few hiccups for the Crimson Tide in its 2009 home finale.

It was 35-0 when Ingram scored with 9:53 remaining in the second quarter. From there, 77 players made their way into a game that was never competitive. Second-ranked Alabama (11-0) rolled to 313 rushing yards while limiting the Mocs (6-5) of the NCAA Football Championship Subdivision to 84 total yards and three interceptions on 48 plays.

"I'm sure there's a lot of things we could have done better," Crimson Tide coach Nick Saban said, "but we ran the ball pretty effectively, got to play a lot of players, and it was good that we didn't have a lot of guys who had to play a whole lot of plays. Maybe that will enhance their recovery for this week."

And you know what's coming this week, don't you?

With the final non-conference game out of the way, Alabama's attention now turns completely to the Iron Bowl at Auburn. The game is six short days away because of CBS' decision to move it to Friday afternoon.

"Those guys, they're going to come out and try to beat us and destroy our dreams," Crimson Tide safety Ali Sharrief said of Auburn. "I know everybody on this team wants to play them and win."

The Tigers were off this weekend, but in many ways it felt like the Crimson Tide was as well.

Heisman Trophy-candidate Ingram compiled 102 yards on 11 carries and did not return after halftime. Neither did starting quarterback Greg McElroy (6 of 11 for 80 yards), wide receiver Julio Jones (except to fair-catch punts) or Alabama's starting offensive line.

Reserves played nearly the entire second half, as Saban made an effort to play all of the 25 seniors on the team who were honored before the kickoff. It was a nice break for the regular contributors.

"I can't say enough about that," left guard Mike Johnson said. "I don't know if people understand how tiring a game actually is, the toll it takes on your body. I don't know how many snaps we got, but it wasn't many.

Alabama quarterback Star Jackson (2) passes in the fourth quarter.

STAFF PHOTO/MARK ALMOND

ap top 10 released 11.22.09

TEAM	1ST	2ND	3RD	4TH	FINAL
ALABAMA	21	14	3	7	45
TENN. CHATTANOOGA	0	0	0	0	0

Attendance   92,012 Bryant-Denny Stadium

SCORING SUMMARY

UA T Richardson 2 yd run (L Tiffin kick) 11 plays, 51 yards, TOP 5:35
UA M Ingram 25 yd run (L Tiffin kick) 2 plays, 69 yards, TOP 0:39
UA J Jones 19 yd pass from G McElroy (L Tiffin kick) 4 plays, 31 yards, TOP 1:53
UA M Ingram 36 yd run (L Tiffin kick), 6 plays, 61 yds, TOP 2:49
UA J Arenas 66 yd punt return (L Tiffin kick)
UA M Ingram 40 yd run (L Tiffin kick) 5 plays, 62 yards, TOP 1:45
UA L Tiffin 41 yd field goal 6 plays, 8 yards, TOP 2:56
UA R Upchurch 21 yd run (J Shelley kick) 8 plays, 72 yards, TOP 4:33

TEAM STATISTICS

	UA	UTC
FIRST DOWNS	26	5
NET YARDS RUSHING	313	48
NET YARDS PASSING	109	36
COMPLETIONS-ATTEMPTS-INT	10-16-0	7-27-3
TOTAL OFFENSE YARDS	422	84
PENALTIES: NUMBER-YARDS	5-61	3-30
PUNTS-YARDS	2-78	7-289
PUNT RETURNS: NUMBER-YDS-TD	2-68-1	0-0-0
KICKOFF RETURNS: NUMBER-YDS-TD	1-12-0	6-144-0
POSSESSION TIME	37:02	22:58
SACKS BY: NUMBER-YARDS LOST	0-0	2-17
FIELD GOALS	1-2	0-0
FUMBLES: NUMBER-LOST	0-0	0-0

INDIVIDUAL OFFENSIVE STATISTICS

RUSHING: UA — M Ingram 11-102; D Goode 11-70, R Upchurch 17-70;
          T Richardson 9-60; G McElroy 2-8; S Jackson 6-3
          UTC — S Kermah 6-18; J.J. Jackson 6-14; Bo Dyer 3-11; C Awuah 6-5
PASSING: UA — G McElroy 11-6-0, 80; S Jackson 5-4-0, 29
          UTC — B.J. Coleman 25-7-2, 36; J Gault 2-0-1, 0
RECEIVING: UA — J Jones 3-65; B Smelley 2-18; M McCoy 2-11; C Peek 1-8;
          B Gibson 1-4, T Richardson 1-3
          UTC — C Pitchford 2-16; J Gault 2-12; B Cooper 2-7; C Awuah 1-1

INDIVIDUAL DEFENSIVE STATISTICS

INTERCEPTIONS: UA — J Arenas 1-22; J Woodall 1-9; C Reamer 1-8
                UTC — None
SACKS: UA —None   UTC — B.J. Taylor 1-0; N Craig 1-0
TACKLES: UA — R McClain 1-6; N Johnson 3-1; J Chapman 1-3;
            J Arenas 2-1; R Lester 2-1
            UTC — S Smigelsky 5-6; J Thornton 4-5; J Tippit 3-6; D Faatiliga 3-4;
            R Consiglio 5-1; J Bradford 3-3; N Craig 2-4

1	2	3	4	5	6	7	8	9	10
FLORIDA	ALABAMA	TEXAS	TCU	CINCINNATI	BOISE STATE	GEORGIA TECH	PITTSBURGH	OHIO STATE	OREGON

"To come out at halftime and kind of turn it over to those guys and kind of watch them blossom into the players that they're going to be over the next few years, it's kind of exciting for us."

Touchdowns on five of Alabama's six possessions build a lead that clearly would not be threatened. Fittingly, much of the Crimson Tide's early accomplishments were credited to seniors playing their final home game.

Seniors Javier Arenas, Cory Reamer and Justin Woodall each intercepted passes. Leigh Tiffin booted a 41-yard field goal, and Arenas provided the highlight of the day with a 66-yard punt return for a touchdown early in the second quarter.

Though Arenas had not reached the end zone on a return this season, it was the seventh punt-return score of his UA career, which set a new SEC record.

"The blocking was spectacular," Arenas said. "A lot of times, I've got to make a decision. 'Should I cut back? Should I do this so this guy can't tackle me?' But they blocked the guys, and it was that much easier."

UTC quarterback B.J. Coleman, a transfer from Tennessee, was harassed consistently by Alabama's pass rush and finished 7 of 25 for 36 yards and two interceptions.

The Mocs drove twice into Crimson Tide territory twice in the first half, but those lone chances at points ended on missed fourth-down attempts.

"You don't kick field goals just because you're at Alabama trying to put three points on the board," UTC coach Russ Huesman said. "That was my whole mindset. Three points wasn't making a big difference. Let's go for it and see what happens."

Alabama backup quarterback Star Jackson threw only five times (completing four), and reserve tailbacks Roy Upchurch and Demetrius Goode combined for 28 carries and 140 yards as Alabama tried to keep the clock moving in the second half.

As a result, the Crimson Tide sustained no serious injuries to key personnel in game No. 11, which might have been the most significant topic heading in games against Auburn and Florida that will decide if the Crimson Tide is destined to play for a national championship after barely missing out on that opportunity last season.

A short week of preparation leads into Friday's trip to Jordan-Hare Stadium, where Alabama has not won in eight years.

"This will be a challenging game for us in every way," Saban said. "It's an important game for everybody that's involved in terms of our program here that we do a good job of getting our players ready to play their best football. Our coaches will do whatever they need to do to get that done."

Arenas Has a Senior Moment

By KEVIN SCARBINSKY

Senior Day takes you out of the moment and into your memories, especially when the Senior Day visitor purrs like a homecoming kitten.

It was easy to let your mind wander during Alabama 45, Chattanooga 0 to consider Alabama's seniors. The ones with tenure have really traveled.

From suffering as Auburn's Iron Bowl streak reached six fingers to savoring Alabama 36, Auburn 0.

From losing to Louisiana-Monroe in 2007 to having a fighting chance to win it all in 2009.

From signing on with Mike Shula to shaping up under Nick Saban.

Don Shula had hard feelings three years ago when Saban left Miami for Tuscaloosa. His son has kept his feelings to himself, then and since, but he didn't depart without leaving some presents behind.

Ten of Alabama's 22 starters Saturday came here while Shula was the head coach. That number jumps to 12 if you count kicker Leigh Tiffin and punter P.J. Fitzgerald, and you should.

For all the good work done by the likes of Mike Johnson on the offensive line and Lorenzo Washington on the defensive front, one of Shula's holdovers stands taller than the rest.

The smartest recruit of the Shula era, and his greatest gift to Saban, was Javier Arenas.

The return man who wants to be known as a cornerback first intercepted a pass in his final home game.

The cornerback who first made a lasting impression as a return man ran a punt back 66 yards for a touchdown.

The high school kid from Tampa who was too small to get more than one SEC scholarship offer - the one he got from Shula and Alabama - just set one SEC record: seven career punt returns for touchdowns.

There will be more. Records, at least, if not touchdowns. Arenas is one good game away from becoming the all-time SEC and NCAA career leader for punt return yardage.

"That's for when you're sitting in the rocking chair, you're old, you act cocky and tell everybody you got the SEC record," Arenas said.

His first thought Saturday after the runback to paydirt wasn't to pat himself on the back. It was: "About time."

See, he hadn't scored on a punt return since the Sugar Bowl.

It's that mentality that has pushed Arenas to play bigger than his size and faster than his speed. As a high school senior, he was a mere three-star recruit. As a college senior, he plays four critical roles for No. 2 Alabama.

He starts at cornerback. He runs back punts and kickoffs. He also plays the "star" position in the nickel package.

Try to name a better 5-foot-9, 195-pound blitzer from the corner.

It was just like Arenas to pick off a pass, break up two more, make three tackles, one behind the line, and run back a punt in his final home game. It was the perfect ending, at least here, to a career full of take-that.

"I don't like to look at it like that," he said. "I've worked hard, and I think it's influenced other people. All it is is giving me momentum for life, to keep working hard, to keep pushing, keep striving, because I can do anything I want to do.

"Like, literally."

Like most of Alabama's starters, Arenas sat out the second half, to rest for the Iron Bowl and beyond. So he had plenty of time to contemplate his final walk off this field in uniform.

But then he actually had to walk off this field in uniform for the final time, and "it kind of hit me."

And then he stopped talking. And then he started feeling a lot of feelings. And then the moment, like him in full flight, passed in a flash.

He started thinking and talking about Auburn.

"If you can't get yourself up for this game," he said, "don't come."

Arenas will be there. Alabama wouldn't be here without him.

(28) DB Javier Arenas and (57) DL Marcell Dareus celebrate an Arenas' sack during the 2009 season.

STAFF PHOTO/GLENN BAESKE

auburn

26
21

Auburn quarterback Chris Todd (12) reaches for a fumble after being sacked by Alabama linebacker Eryk Anders (32) in the second quarter . Alabama defensive lineman Lorenzo Washington (97) charges in. Anders recovered the ball.

STAFF PHOTO/MARK ALMOND

CRIMSON TIDE
TIGERS
11.27.09 | 1:30 p.m. | Jordan-Hare Stadium

Top-Ranked Defense Catches Up to Tigers

By MIKE HERNDON

Alabama was only 10 minutes into Friday's Iron Bowl and its top-ranked defense was already on its heels.

With little to lose, the Tigers pulled out all the stops on their first two possessions. They opened the scoring with a 67-yard reverse by Terrell Zachery, then recovered a gutsy onside kick and used a 22-yard completion on a double pass from Chris Todd to Darvin Adams to set up Todd's 1-yard scoring pass to Eric Smith.

It wasn't unexpected. But that didn't mean Alabama could stop it.

"I knew it would be tough at the start," Crimson Tide coach Nick Saban said. "When these guys go off the script, they have all kinds of formations, all kinds of plays — double passes, reverse passes and all kinds of stuff. Most of it is stuff you haven't seen before."

The UA defense, whose average of 225 yards allowed per game was the lowest in the country entering the game, did just that. The Crimson Tide, which had allowed opponents to gain more than 300 yards only twice entering Friday's game, gave up 332 yards but allowed only one touchdown after the Tigers' first-quarter blitz, giving its offense time to rally for a 26-21 victory.

"They threw everything they had at us," Alabama linebacker Cory Reamer said. "We knew they were going to do something different that we've never seen before. We expect that every week now, especially with all these teams we've faced who have had a week off before they play us."

After allowing 149 yards in the first quarter and 193 in the first half, Alabama gave up only 139 in the final two quarters. Seventy-two of those yards came on the Tigers' lone second-half touchdown, a bomb that Darvin Adams caught behind the Crimson Tide secondary when Todd caught Alabama in a corner blitz.

Adams' touchdown was the longest pass play allowed by UA since 1999, and Zachary's first-quarter reverse was the longest run the Crimson Tide has allowed since 2005.

"I think the biggest thing is the players settled down," Saban said. "Like on the reverse, we rotated the coverage the wrong way and we had no run support over there. They motioned a guy in the backfield, which we should have gone from one rotation to the other and we didn't do it. So it's just a matter of all that stuff they see, making the proper adjustments.

"They (Auburn) did a good job of executing. I don't want to take anything away from them. But we didn't always play it exactly right, and it was their formation variations that probably created some of the mistakes."

"We all huddled up every time before we ran out (in the second half) and we talked about: This is the time for us to step up," Reamer said. "It's on our shoulders. We executed when we needed to. We blew a lot of assignments today, which is unfortunate. We did not play our best football, but we played well enough to get the win."

Alabama defensive back Javier Arenas (28) sacks Auburn quarterback Chris Todd (12).

STAFF PHOTO/FRANK COUCH

ap top 10 released 11.29.09

TEAM	1ST	2ND	3RD	4TH	FINAL
ALABAMA	0	14	6	6	26
AUBURN	14	0	7	0	21

Attendance   87,451 Jordan-Hare Stadium

SCORING SUMMARY

AU T Zachery 67 yd run (W Byrum kick) 4 plays, 80 yards, TOP 1:42
AU E Smith 1 yd pass from C Todd (W Byrum kick) 12 plays, 58 yards, TOP 5:58
UA T Richardson 2 yd run (L Tiffin kick) 10 plays, 58 yards, TOP 4:11
UA C Peek 33 yd pass from G McElroy (L Tiffin kick) 5 plays, 45 yards, TOP 2:18
AU D Adams 72 yd pass from C Todd (W Byrum kick) 2 plays, 76 yards, TOP 0:47
UA L Tiffin 27 yd field goal 5 plays, 23 yards, TOP 1:25
UA L Tiffin 31 yd field goal 7 plays, 30 yards, TOP 4:24
UA R Upchurch 4 yd pass from G McElroy 15 plays, 79 yards, TOP 7:03

TEAM STATISTICS

	UA	AU
FIRST DOWNS	17	15
NET YARDS RUSHING	73	151
NET YARDS PASSING	218	181
COMPLETIONS-ATTEMPTS-INT	21-32-0	15-27-1
TOTAL OFFENSE YARDS	291	332
PENALTIES: NUMBER-YARDS	4-26	8-68
PUNTS-YARDS	5-226	8-320
PUNT RETURNS: NUMBER-YDS-TD	2-67-0	2-5-0
KICKOFF RETURNS: NUMBER-YDS-TD	1-46-0	4-99-0
POSSESSION TIME	33:47	26:13
SACKS BY: NUMBER-YARDS LOST	3-32	3-7
FIELD GOALS	2-3	0-0
FUMBLES: NUMBER-LOST	1-0	2-1

INDIVIDUAL OFFENSIVE STATISTICS

RUSHING: UA – T Richardson 15-51; M Ingram 16-30; G McElroy 4-0
           AU – T Zachery 1-67; B Tate 18-54; O McCalebb 5-24; M Fannin 1-14
PASSING: UA – G McElroy 31-21-0, 218; M Ingram 1-0-0, 0
           AU – C Todd 25-15-1, 181; K Burns 1-0-0, 0
RECEIVING: UA – J Jones 9-83; C Peek 3-53; T Richardson 3-31; M Ingram 3-21;
           R Upchurch 2-15; D Hanks 1-15
           AU – D Adams 4-138, M Fannin 4-20, B Tate 4-17; E Blake 1-7,
           E Smith 1-1, T Zachery 1 -2

INDIVIDUAL DEFENSIVE STATISTICS

INTERCEPTIONS: UA – M Barron 1-14
                AU – None
SACKS: UA –R McClain 1-0; J Arenas 1-0; E Anders 1-0
         AU – A Coleman 1-1; J Ricks 0-1; M Blanc 0-1; N Fairley 0-1
TACKLES: UA – R McClain 4-8; E Anders 4-3; J Arenas 4-3; Justin Woodall 3-2;
           Kareem Jackson 3-2; Ali Sharrief 2-3
           AU – J Bynes 7-3; J Evans 8-0; N Thorpe 7-1; D Bates 5-2; C Stevens 3-3

Auburn Pushes Bama to Brink of Diasaster

Alabama running back Trent Richardson (3) drags Auburn linebacker Jonathan Evans (35) in the second quarter.

STAFF PHOTO/MARK ALMOND

By GENTRY ESTES

When the roars finally died, all that remained were those in crimson, celebrating through the cold as if second-ranked Alabama had steamrolled Auburn like seemingly everyone had forecast.

Since when is an Iron Bowl ever that predictable?

While Alabama defensive end Luther Davis held up two fingers and quarterback Greg McElroy pointed to fans like a rock star in an encore, the reality of this Friday was best described by a brief head shake and one word by exhausted Crimson Tide de-

fensive coordinator Kirby Smart as he exited Jordan-Hare Stadium:

"Whew."

"We did survive," Alabama coach Nick Saban said, "because of our character and our resiliency. You've got to win games like that, and I'm proud of our team for the way they did it."

Alabama's only lead on this day will stand always in the record books, another memorable chapter in a storied rivalry. And, yes, Friday's 26-21 victory keeps it unde-feated and in the hunt for a national title heading into next weekend's SEC title game against top-ranked Florida.

The Crimson Tide (12-0, 8-0 SEC) got what it wanted, and in a way so did the Tigers (7-5, 3-5), who regained pride after last year's blowout in Tuscaloosa. This time, Alabama certainly earned it.

The upset that would have turned the tables of the state's football pecking order and crushed Alabama's dreams was there to behold. It grew more tangible by the minute for the 87,451 hanging on every whistle, the frenzied souls wearing orange and blue and those in crimson who could see a horrific end to the 2009 magic materializing in an odd game that had progressed like seemingly no one thought it would.

Auburn's offense hit the nation's No. 1 defense for the two longest touchdowns of the Saban era at Alabama. The Tigers' overmatched run defense stoned Alabama's Heisman Trophy candidate Mark Ingram for just 30 yards on 16 carries. Overall, AU outgained the Crimson Tide 332 yards to 291 and leapt to a 14-0 lead behind trick plays and an onside kick in the opening moments.

"They always have some trick plays and executed on every single one of them, it seemed like," Alabama linebacker Cory Reamer said. "They threw everything in the book at us in the first half."

The Tigers clutched a 21-20 advantage entering the fourth quarter. It remained that way until the 8:27 mark, when the Crimson Tide, star-studded yet staggered, took over at its 21-yard line and showed everyone why it will play a week from today for a spot in the BCS title game.

Saban called it "one of the greatest drives I've ever been associated with."

"As you looked in the huddle, from a quarterback's perspective, I'm always looking and everyone is looking at me, there was no sense of worry, no sense of panic," McElroy said. "We were able to take care of business, and everyone knew we were going to. Everyone knew we could if we just executed."

It took 14 plays and nearly seven minutes for Alabama to reach Auburn's 4. There were six consecutive completions by McElroy, and two third-down conversions.

Another one loomed: A third-and-3 that begged for a running play to set up a field goal that would have amounted to an extra point and reclaim the lead with the clock nearing 90 seconds. Crimson Tide offensive coordinator Jim McElwain, in fact, did call a plunge by Trent Richardson into the line to set up place-kicker Leigh Tiffin.

But no, Saban thought. That's what they'd be expecting. So he called timeout. On a headset on the sideline, senior tailback Roy Upchurch screamed "Cody-five! Cody-five!" — the formation where

nose tackle Terrence Cody enters on offense.

Saban combined the two, sending in Cody (which always means a run) and calling a pass to Upchurch. Alabama had never run the play out of that formation in a game.

"I really didn't want to just play for a field goal," Saban said. "I guess I tried to talk them into throwing a pass. Then when we got out there and lined up, I wanted to throw a pass. ... We got in the goal-line formation and made them think we were going to run."

McElroy faked a handoff, rolled right and lobbed a pass to Upchurch, who was in the end zone, steps from Auburn's Neiko Thorpe.

It was the first touchdown catch of Upchurch's career, a fitting moment for a senior who has battled injuries and off-the-field issues, maintaining all along that something good was waiting in the end.

"Hey, I've got a story to tell," Upchurch said. "I didn't know it would be this big. Patience, that's been the big thing with me all year, and it paid off."

Receiver Julio Jones caught four passes on the critical drive, ending with a career-high nine catches for 83 yards. McElroy finished 21-of-31 passing for 218 yards and two touchdowns.

Auburn quarterback Chris Todd, who was 15 of 25 for 181 yards and two TDs, drove the Tigers 38 yards in response to the final score, leaving one second to heave a pass into the end zone. But the ball was knocked down to begin Alabama's latest celebration.

But this one felt different. In that moment of relief and exaltation, the Crimson Tide knew it had won at Auburn for the first time since 2001.

"I know with fans and other people, everything's based on the results," Saban said. "But great competitors can play in that moment and that time, and great teams can play in that moment and that time. I'm not saying we have a great team. I'm just saying that our team was able to do that tonight, and that was important in us finishing this game like we needed to get the win."

Cody-5 Keeps Perfect Season Alive

By PAUL GATTIS

The play is called Cody-5, and Roy Upchurch was begging loudly for the coaching staff to call it.

"I was yelling and screaming," Upchurch said. "They just said my number and I went out and did it."

Cody-5 is the play Alabama's coaching staff called for the winning touchdown. The Tide lined up in a goal-line formation with defensive tackle Terrence Cody playing his role as a fullback/blocker.

But instead of running the ball - as Alabama has done all season out of that formation - quarterback Greg McElroy faked a handoff, rolled right and fired a quick pass to Upchurch for the touchdown.

Cody-5. As in Terrence Cody and Upchurch's jersey number is 5.

"Hey, if Daniel Moore wants to make a painting of it, I'm his man," Upchurch said.

Such an unlikely star in such a big game, Upchurch - a senior from Tallahassee, Fla. - had touched the ball just once in Alabama's previous 66 plays. He's the third-string tailback who has battled injuries throughout his career.

"I was just ready," he said. "I was just ready to get in the end zone, put points on the board and get out of here."

On third-and-3 at the Auburn 4, Alabama originally called a running play. And if it didn't result in a touchdown, Leigh Tiffin could kick a short field goal for the lead.

But coach Nick Saban didn't want a field goal. He called a timeout, told his coaches he wanted to throw a pass and somebody finally heard Upchurch screaming for "Cody-5."

"As soon as I got the play call I was like 'We're gonna throw it?' " McElroy said. "But I loved the play call. It was something we'd really been hitting on."

As Upchurch ran his route, he said an Auburn defender grabbed his facemask and "I was just panicking. I had to find (the ball) and I put it away."

Until that pass, Alabama had run 812 plays this season and Upchurch had touched the ball on just 50 of them. Playing behind Mark Ingram and freshman sensation Trent Richardson, Upchurch's opportunities were rare.

But Upchurch's last touch in his last regular-season game, may be immortalized by Moore.

"It doesn't get any bigger, really, than scoring the winning touchdown for the Iron Bowl," senior Brandon Deaderick said. "He did a great job when he got his opportunity. He really shined."

Alabama defenders, from left, Justin Woodall (27), Kareem Jackson (3), Eryk Anders (32), Rolando McClain (25) and Terrence Cody (62)
STAFF PHOTO/MARK ALMOND

ALABAMA'S FINAL SEASON STATISTICS*

OFFENSE

RUSHING

	GP	ATT	GAIN	LOSS	NET	AVG	TD	LG	AVG/G
Mark Ingram	13	249	1562	20	1542	6.2	15	70	118.6
T. Richardson	13	126	669	27	642	5.1	6	52	49.4
Roy Upchurch	12	46	304	14	290	6.3	2	34	24.2
Terry Grant	8	40	179	13	166	4.2	3	42	20.8
Demetrius Goode	10	16	108	0	108	6.8	0	14	10.8
Greg McElroy	13	47	176	66	110	2.3	1	16	8.5

PASSING

	GP	EFFIC	COMP	ATT	INT	PCT	YDS	TD	LG	AVG/G
Greg McElroy	13	142.01	192	314	4	61.1	2450	17	80	188.5
Star Jackson	5	126.36	13	18	0	72.2	116	0	21	23.2

RECEIVING

	GP	NO.	YDS	AVG	TD	LG	AVG/G
Julio Jones	12	42	573	13.6	4	73	47.8
Mark Ingram	13	30	322	10.7	3	69	24.8
Marquis Maze	13	30	519	17.3	2	80	39.9
Colin Peek	13	26	313	12.0	3	33	24.1
Darius Hanks	13	17	272	16.0	3	45	20.9
T. Richardson	13	14	107	7.6	0	17	8.2
Roy Upchurch	12	12	72	6.0	1	14	6.0
Mike McCoy	12	10	149	14.9	1	35	12.4
Brad Smelley	12	7	50	7.1	0	11	4.2
Earl Alexander	13	4	52	13.0	0	21	4.0

DEFENSE

DEFENSE LEADERS

	GP	UA	A	TOTAL	TFL	SACK	INT	PBU
Rolando McClain	13	51	50	101	12.5	4.0	2	5
Javier Arenas	12	43	23	66	12.0	5.0	3	4
Mark Barron	13	38	32	70	2.5	0.5	7	10
Eryk Anders	13	26	33	59	12.5	5.0	1	1
Cory Reamer	13	26	21	47	7.0	2.0	1	3
Justin Woodall	13	28	15	43	1.5	0	3	5
Kareem Jackson	13	28	18	46	3.0	0	1	12
Marcell Dareus	13	19	13	32	9.0	6.5	0	2
Marquis Johnson	13	23	5	28	1.0	0	1	16
Nico Johnson	11	16	11	27	4.5	1.0	0	2
Terrence Cody	13	11	14	25	6.0	0	0	1
Robby Green	13	18	9	27	0.0	0	1	6
Brandon Deaderick	13	9	13	22	4.5	1.0	0	0
Ali Sharrief	13	11	10	21	0.0	0	0	0
Tyrone King	13	8	10	18	1.5	1.5	0	0
Lorenzo Washington	13	11	8	19	4.0	2.0	0	1
Dont'a Hightower	4	5	11	16	4.0	1.0	0	1
Courtney Upshaw	13	7	7	14	1.0	1.0	0	0
Josh Chapman	12	3	11	14	2.5	0.5	0	0
Chris Jordan	12	10	2	12	0.0	0	0	0
Luther Davis	13	3	8	11	1.5	0	0	0

DEFENSE

DEFENSE LEADERS

	GP	UA	A	TOTAL	TFL	SACK	INT	PBU
Chris Rogers	13	9	1	10	0.0	0	0	1
Robert Lester	7	6	2	8	0.0	0	0	0
Nick Gentry	4	0	7	7	0.0	0	0	0
Dre Kirkpatrick	11	3	4	7	0.0	0	0	0
T. Richardson	13	4	2	6	0.0	0	0	0
Rod Woodson	11	3	2	5	0.0	0	0	0
Jerrell Harris	5	1	2	3	0.0	0	0	0
Kerry Murphy	5	0	3	3	0.0	0	0	0
Chavis Williams	7	1	1	2	0.0	0	0	0
Roy Upchurch	12	1	1	2	0.0	0	0	0
Leigh Tiffin	13	1	1	2	0.0	0	0	0
Terry Grant	8	1	1	2	0.0	0	0	0
Milton Talbert	1	0	1	1	0.0	0	0	0
Greg McElroy	13	0	1	1	0.0	0	0	0
Colin Peek	13	1	0	1	0.0	0	0	0
Alex Watkins	4	0	1	1	0.0	0	0	0
Damion Square	2	0	1	1	0.5	0	0	0
Marquis Maze	13	1	0	1	0.0	0	0	0
Julio Jones	12	1	0	1	0.0	0	0	0
P. J. Fitzgerald	13	2	0	2	0.0	0	0	0
Brian Selman	13	0	1	1	0.0	0	0	0
Hampton Gray	1	1	0	1	0.0	0	0	0
James Carpenter	13	1	0	1	0.0	0	0	0
Darius Hanks	13	0	0	0	0.0	0	0	0

INTERCEPTIONS

	NO.	YDS	AVG	TD	LG
Mark Barron	7	125	17.9	1	77
Justin Woodall	3	33	11.0	0	24
Javier Arenas	3	22	7.3	0	22
Rolando McClain	2	21	10.5	0	21
Eryk Anders	1	0	0.0	0	0
Marquis Johnson	1	0	0.0	0	0
Cory Reamer	1	8	8.0	0	8
Robby Green	1	0	0.0	0	0
Kareem Jackson	1	79	79.0	0	79

FUMBLE RETURNS

	NO.	YDS	AVG	TD	LG
Courtney Upshaw	1	45	45.0	1	45

ALABAMA'S FINAL SEASON STATISTICS*

SPECIAL TEAMS

FIELD GOALS

	ATT	GOOD	LONG	BLOCKED
Leigh Tiffin	33	29	50	0
Jeremy Shelley	1	0	0	0

PUNTING

	NO.	YDS	AVG	LG	BLOCKED
P. J. Fitzgerald	51	2146	42.1	55	0

KICKOFFS

	NO.	YDS	AVG	TB	OB
Leigh Tiffin	87	5558	63.9	13	2
Jeremy Shelley	1	57	57.0	0	0
P. J. Fitzgerald	1	55	55.0	0	0

PUNT RETURNS

	NO.	YDS	AVG	TD	LG
Javier Arenas	29	474	16.3	1	66
Julio Jones	5	75	15.0	0	33
Lorenzo Washington	1	16	16.0	0	0
Cory Reamer	1	3	3.0	0	0

KICK RETURNS

	NO.	YDS	AVG	TD	LG
Javier Arenas	19	551	29.0	0	61
Terry Grant	8	176	22.0	0	30
T. Richardson	1	20	20.0	0	20
Damion Square	1	5	5.0	0	5
Julio Jones	1	12	12.0	0	12
Baron Huber	1	10	10.0	0	10

TEAM GAME HIGHS

Rushes	56	vs Chattanooga (Nov 21, 2009)
Yards Rushing	313	vs Chattanooga (Nov 21, 2009)
Yards Per Rush	6.9	vs South Carolina (Oct 17, 2009)
TD Rushes	5	vs North Texas (Sept 19, 2009)
Pass Attempts	35	at Mississippi (Oct 10, 2009)
Pass Completions	22	vs North Texas (Sept 19, 2009)
Yards Passing	291	vs Arkansas (Sept 26, 2009)
Yards Per Pass	13.3	vs Florida (Dec 5, 2009)
TD Passes	3	vs Arkansas (Sept 26, 2009)
Total Plays	79	vs Virginia Tech (Sept 5, 2009)
Total Offense	523	vs North Texas (Sept 19, 2009)
Yards Per Play	7.8	vs Fla. International (Sept 12, 2009)
Points	53	vs North Texas (Sept 19, 2009)
Sacks By	5	vs Virginia Tech (Sept 5, 2009)
	5	vs Fla. International (Sept 12, 2009)
	5	vs South Carolina (Oct 17, 2009)
First Downs	28	vs North Texas (Sept 19, 2009)
Penalties	10	vs Virginia Tech (Sept 5, 2009)
	10	vs South Carolina (Oct 17, 2009)
Penalty Yards	113	vs South Carolina (Oct 17, 2009)
Turnovers	4	vs South Carolina (Oct 17, 2009)
Interceptions By	4	at Mississippi (Oct 10, 2009)

INDIVIDUAL GAME HIGHS

Rushes	28	Mark Ingram at Mississippi (Oct 10, 2009)
	28	Mark Ingram vs Florida (Dec 5, 2009)
Yards Rushing	246	Mark Ingram vs South Carolina (Oct 17, 2009)
TD Rushes	3	Mark Ingram vs Florida (Dec 5, 2009)
Long Rush	70	Mark Ingram at Mississippi State (Nov 14, 2009)
Pass Attempts	34	Greg McElroy at Mississippi (Oct 10, 2009)
	34	Greg McElroy vs LSU (Nov 7, 2009)
Pass Completions	21	Greg McElroy at Auburn (Nov 27, 2009)
Yards Passing	291	Greg McElroy vs Arkansas (Sept 26, 2009)
TD Passes	3	Greg McElroy vs Arkansas (Sept 26, 2009)
Long Pass	80	Greg McElroy vs Arkansas (Sept 26, 2009)
Receptions	9	Julio Jones at Auburn (Nov 27, 2009)
Yards Receiving	102	Julio Jones vs LSU (Nov 7, 2009)
TD Receptions	1	Mark Ingram vs Virginia Tech (Sept 5, 2009)
	1	Mike McCoy vs Fla. International (Sept 12, 2009)
	1	Marquis Maze vs North Texas (Sept 19, 2009)
	1	Mark Ingram vs North Texas (Sept 19, 2009)
	1	Marquis Maze vs Arkansas (Sept 26, 2009)
	1	Julio Jones vs Arkansas (Sept 26, 2009)
	1	Mark Ingram vs Arkansas (Sept 26, 2009)
	1	Colin Peek at Kentucky (Oct 3, 2009)
	1	Darius Hanks at Kentucky (Oct 3, 2009)
	1	Julio Jones vs LSU (Nov 7, 2009)
	1	Darius Hanks vs LSU (Nov 7, 2009)
	1	Julio Jones at Mississippi State (Nov 14, 2009)
	1	Darius Hanks at Mississippi State (Nov 14, 2009)
	1	Julio Jones vs Chattanooga (Nov 21, 2009)
	1	Colin Peek at Auburn (Nov 27, 2009)
	1	Roy Upchurch at Auburn (Nov 27, 2009)
	1	Colin Peek vs Florida (Dec 5, 2009)
Long Reception	80	Marquis Maze vs Arkansas (Sept 26, 2009)
Field Goals	5	Leigh Tiffin at Mississippi (Oct 10, 2009)
Long Field Goal	50	Leigh Tiffin vs Tennessee (Oct 24, 2009)
Punts	7	P. J. Fitzgerald vs Arkansas (Sept 26, 2009)
Punting Average	49.0	P. J. Fitzgerald vs North Texas (Sept 19, 2009)
Long Punt	55	P. J. Fitzgerald vs Chattanooga (Nov 21, 2009)
	55	P. J. Fitzgerald at Auburn (Nov 27, 2009)
Long Punt Return	66	Javier Arenas vs Chattanooga (Nov 21, 2009)
Long Kickoff Return	61	Javier Arenas vs North Texas (Sept 19, 2009)
Tackles	14	Javier Arenas vs Tennessee (Oct 24, 2009)
Sacks	2.0	Rolando McClain vs Virginia Tech (Sept 5, 2009)
	2.0	Marcell Dareus vs Fla. International (Sept 12, 2009)
	2.0	Javier Arenas vs Arkansas (Sept 26, 2009)
	2.0	Marcell Dareus vs LSU (Nov 7, 2009)
Tackles For Loss	4.5	Javier Arenas vs Tennessee (Oct 24, 2009)
Interceptions	2	Mark Barron at Mississippi State (Nov 14, 2009)

*Through the SEC Championship Game (December 5, 2009).

2009 ALABAMA ROSTER

NO	NAME	POS	Year	HT/WT	Hometown (Last School)
1	B.J. Scott	DB	SO	5-11/188	Prichard, Ala. (Vigor)
1	Chris Rogers	DB	SR	6-0/195	Lakeland, Fla. (Evangel Christian)
2	Star Jackson	QB	FR	6-3/195	Lake Worth, Fla. (Lake Worth)
2	Tana Patrick	LB	FR	6-3/235	Bridgeport, Ala. (North Jackson)
3	Trent Richardson	RB	FR	5-11/220	Pensacola, Fla. (Escambia)
3	Kareem Jackson	DB	JR	5-11/192	Macon, Ga. (Fork Union Military)
4	Mark Barron	DB	SO	6-2/215	Mobile, Ala. (St. Paul's)
4	Marquis Maze	WR	SO	5-10/179	Tarrant, Ala. (Tarrant)
5	Roy Upchurch	RB	SR	6-0/205	Tallahassee, Fla. (Godby)
6	Demetrius Goode	RB	SO	5-10/190	LaGrange, Ga. (Hargrave)
7	Kenny Bell	WB	FR	6-1/160	Rayville, La. (Rayville)
7	P.J. Fitzgerald	P	SR	5-11/198	Coral Springs, Fla. (Stoneman Douglas)
8	Julio Jones	WR	SO	6-4/210	Foley, Ala. (Foley)
9	Phelon Jones	DB		5-11/195	Moblie, Ala. (LSU)
9	Nick Williams	WR	FR	5-10/165	Fort Lauderdale, Fla. (St. Thomas Aquinas)
10	Jerrell Harris	LB	SO	6-3/215	Gadsden, Ala. (Gadsden City)
10	A.J. McCarron	QB	FR	6-4/190	Mobile, Ala. (Saint Paul's)
10	Morgan Ogilvie	QB	SO	6-0/185	Mountain Brook, Ala. (Mountain Brook)
11	Brandon Gibson	WR	SO	6-1/196	Mobile, Ala. (UMS-Wright)
12	Greg McElroy	QB	JR	6-3/220	Southlake, Texas (Carroll)
13	Rob Ezell	WR	JR	5-10/170	Athens, Ala. (Athens)
13	Cory Reamer	LB	SR	6-4/234	Hoover, Ala. (Hoover)
15	Darius Hanks	WR	JR	6-0/172	Norcross, Ga. (Norcross)
16	Thomas Darrah	QB	SO	6-6/212	Newnan, Ga. (Newnan)
17	Brad Smelley	TE	SO	6-3/218	Tuscaloosa, Ala. (American Christian)
18	Rod Woodson	DB	FR	5-11/200	Olive Branch, Miss. (Olive Branch)
20	Tyrone King	DB	SR	5-11/198	Birmingham, Ala. (Grambling State)
21	Dre Kirkpatrick	DB	FR	6-3/185	Gadsden, Ala. (Gadsden City)
22	Mark Ingram	RB	SO	5-10/215	Flint, Mich. (Southwestern Academy)
23	Robby Green	DB	SO	6-0/180	New Orleans, La. (John Curtis Christian)
24	Marquis Johnson	DB	SR	5-11/192	Sarasota, Fla. (Booker)
25	Rolando McClain	LB	JR	6-4/258	Decatur, Ala. (Decatur)
26	Ali Sharrief	DB	SR	5-9/205	Stevenson, Ala. (North Jackson)
27	Justin Woodall	DB	SR	6-2/220	Oxford, Miss. (Lafayette HS)
28	Javier Arenas	DB	SR	5-9/198	Tampa, Fla. (Robinson)
29	Terry Grant	RB	JR	5-9/190	Lumberton, Miss. (Lumberton)
30	Dont'a Hightower	LB	SO	6-4/250	Lewisburg, Tenn. (Marshall County)
32	Eryk Anders	LB	SR	6-2/227	San Antonio, Tex. (Smithson Valley)
33	Hampton Gray	DB	SR	5-1/194	Tuscaloosa, Ala. (Tuscaloosa County)
33	Mike Marrow	RB	FR	6-2/240	Holland, Ohio (Central Catholic)
34	Jeramie Griffin	RB	SO	6-2/228	Batesville, Miss. (South Panola)
35	Nico Johnson	LB	FR	6-3/225	Andalusia, Ala. (Andalusia)
36	Chris Jordan	LB	SO	6-2/220	Brentwood, Tenn. (Brentwood Academy)
37	Robert Lester	DB	FR	6-2/210	Foley, Ala. (Foley)
39	Kyle Pennington	DB	JR	5-11/177	Chatom, Ala. (Washington County)
40	DeMarcus DuBose	LB	SO	6-1/230	Montgomery, Ala. (Jefferson Davis)
40	Baron Huber	RB/ TE	SR	6-3/249	Knoxville, Tenn. (Powell)
41	Courtney Upshaw	LB	SO	6-2/249	Eufaula, Ala. (Eufaula)
41	Jacob Vane	RB	SR	6-0/228	Oak Ridge, Tenn. (Oak Ridge)
42	Eddie Lacy	RB	FR	6-0/210	Geismar, La. (Dutchtown)
44	Alex Benson	LB	SR	6-1/210	Trussville, Ala. (Hewitt-Trussville)
46	Wesley Neighbors	DB	SO	6-1/210	Huntsville, Ala. (Huntsville)
46	William Strickland	WR	SO	5-10/173	Tuscaloosa, Ala. (Northridge)
47	Ed Stinson	DL/LB	FR	6-4/240	Homestead, Fla. (South Dade)
48	Travis Sikes	WR	JR	6-2/188	Nashville, Tenn. (Christ Presbyterian)
49	Jonathan Atchison	LB	FR	6-2/235	Atlanta, Ga. (Douglass)
50	Brian Selman	SNP	SR	6-0/211	Vestavia Hills, Ala. (Vestavia Hills)
51	Michael DeJohn	LB	JR	6-0/220	Hoover, Ala. (Hoover)
52	Alfred McCullough	OL	SO	6-2/292	Athens, Ala. (Athens)
54	Glenn Harbin	DL	SO	6-6/245	Mobile, Ala. (McGill-Toolen)
54	Russell Raines	OL	FR	6-2/290	Satsuma, Ala. (Satsuma)
55	Chavis Williams	LB	JR	6-4/223	Dora, Ala. (Dora)
56	William Ming	DL	FR	6-3/260	Athens, Ala. (Athens)
57	Marcell Dareus	DL	SO	6-3/280	Huffman, Ala. (Huffman)
58	Nick Gentry	DL	SO	6-1/254	Prattville, Ala. (Prattville)
59	Brandon Moore	DL	FR	6-5/310	Montgomery, Ala. (Carver)
60	David Williams	OL	FR	6-3/272	Duncanville, Ala. (Hillcrest)
61	Carson Tinker	ST	SO	6-1/230	Murfreesboro, Tenn. (Riverdale)
61	Anthony Steen	OL-DL	FR	6-3/305	Lambert, Miss. (Lee Academy)
62	Terrence Cody	DL	SR	6-5/365	Ft. Myers, Fla. (Gulf Coast C.C.)
63	Kellen Williams	OL	FR	6-3/290	Lawrenceville, Ga. (Brookwood)
64	Kerry Murphy	DL	FR	6-4/323	Hoover, Ala. (Hargrave/Hoover)
65	Chance Warmack	OL	FR	6-3/301	Atlanta, Ga. (Westlake)
65	Allen Skelton	OL	SO	6-1/256	Coker, Ala. (Tuscaloosa County)
66	Brian Motley	OL	JR	6-2/289	Autaugaville, Ala. (Autaugaville)
67	John Michael Boswell	OL	SO	6-5/300	Northport, Ala. (Tuscaloosa County)
68	Taylor Pharr	OL	JR	6-6/290	Irondale, Ala. (Shades Valley)
72	Tyler Love	OL	FR	6-7/290	Mountain Brook, Ala. (Mountain Brook)
73	William Vlachos	OL	SO	6-1/294	Birmingham, Ala. (Mountain Brook)
74	David Ross	OL	JR	6-3/295	Homewood, Ala. (Homewood)
75	Barrett Jones	OL	SO	6-5/280	Memphis, Tenn. (Evangelical Christian)
76	D.J. Fluker	OL	FR	6-6/340	Foley, Ala. (Foley)
77	James Carpenter	OL	JR	6-5/300	Augusta, Ga. (Hephzibah)
78	Mike Johnson	OL	SR	6-6/305	Pensacola, Fla. (Pine Forest)
79	Drew Davis	OL	SR	6-7/305	Evergreen, Ala. (Sparta Academy)
80	Mike McCoy	WR	SR	6-3/215	Rankin, Miss. (Northwest Rankin)
81	Kendall Kelly	WR	FR	6-3/216	Gadsden, Ala. (Gadsden City)
82	Earl Alexander	WR	JR	6-4/216	Phenix City, Ala. (Central)
83	Kevin Norwood	WR	FR	6-2/180	D'Iberville, Miss. (D'Iberville)
84	Colin Peek	TE	SR	6-6/255	Ponte Vedra, Fla. (Georgia Tech)
85	Preston Dial	TE	JR	6-3/245	Mobile, Ala. (UMS-Wright)
86	Undra Billingsley	TE	FR	6-3/275	Birmingham, Ala. (Woodlawn)
87	Drew Bullard	LB	RS SO	6-3/240	Florence, Ala. (Florence)
87	Chris Underwood	TE	SO	6-4/231	Birmingham, Ala. (Vestavia Hills)
88	Michael Bowman	WR	FR	6-4/210	Rossville, Ga. (Ridgeland)
89	Michael Williams	TE	FR	6-6/266	Reform, Ala. (Pickens County)
90	Milton Talbert	DL	JR	6-4/275	Hattiesburg, Miss. (Hattiesburg)
91	Alex Watkins	LB	SO	6-3/225	Brownsville, Tenn. (Haywood)
92	Damion Square	DL	RS FR	6-3/273	Houston, Tex. (Yates)
93	Chris Bonds	DL	FR	6-4/280	Columbia, S.C. (Richland Northeast)
94	Darrington Sentimore	DL	FR	6-3/280	Norco, La. (Destrehan)
94	Jeremy Shelley	PK	FR	5-10/170	Raleigh, N.C. (Broughton)
95	Colin Gallagher	PK	JR	6-0/180	Atlanta, Ga. (Marist)
95	Brandon Deaderick	DL	SR	6-4/287	Elizabethtown, Ky. (Elizabethtown)
96	Luther Davis	DL	JR	6-3/299	West Monroe, La. (West Monroe)
97	Lorenzo Washington	DL	SR	6-5/290	Loganville, Ga. (Hargrave Military)
98	Heath Thomas	P	SR	6-3/213	Montgomery, Ala. (Trinity Presbyterian)
99	Josh Chapman	DL	SO	6-1/305	Hoover, Ala. (Hoover)
99	Leigh Tiffin	K	SR	6-2/212	Muscle Shoals, Ala. (Muscle Shoals)